Dear Reader:

The book you are about to read is the latest bestseller from the St. Martin's True Crime Library, the imprint the *New York Times* calls "the leader in true crime!" Each month, we offer you a fascinating account of the latest, most sensational crime that has captured the national attention. St. Martin's is the publisher of perennial bestselling true crime author Jack Olsen, whose SALT OF THE EARTH is the true story of one woman's triumph over life-shattering violence; Joseph Wambaugh called it "powerful and absorbing." Fannie Weinstein and Melinda Wilson tell the story of a beautiful honors student who was lured into the hidden world of sex for hire in THE COED CALL GIRL MURDER. St. Martin's is also proud to publish two-time Edgar Award-winning author Carlton Stowers, whose TO THE LAST BREATH recounts a two-year-old girl's mysterious death, and the dogged investigation that led loved ones to the most unlikely murderer: her own father. The book you now hold, MURDER IN HOLLYWOOD by Gary C. King, gives you the up-to-date story on a celebrated case that has riveted the nation.

St. Martin's True Crime Library gives you the stories *behind* the headlines. Our authors take you right to the scene of the crime and into the minds of the most notorious murderers to show you what really makes them tick. St. Martin's True Crime Library paperbacks are better than the most terrifying thriller, because it's all true! The next time you want a crackling good read, make sure it's got the St. Martin's True Crime Library logo on the spine—you'll be up all night!

Charles E. Spicer, Jr.
Executive Editor, St. Martin's True Crime Library

SOMETIME BETWEEN 9:30 AND 9:40 P.M., BLAKE AND Bonny left Vitello's and together walked back to the black Stealth. After letting Bonny into the car, Blake realized that he had left a handgun at the restaurant. He had begun carrying it recently because of Bonny's fear for her safety. He told her that he would be right back and purportedly walked back to Vitello's to retrieve it.

When he returned to the car minutes later he found Bonny slumped over in the passenger seat, unconscious and bleeding from a wound to her head. Unable to revive her, Blake ran to the home of filmmaker Sean Stanek, located directly behind Vitello's and just across the street from the car. This marked the beginning of a case that would rock Hollywood like it hadn't been rocked since the O. J. Simpson trial. . . .

St. Martin's Paperbacks
True Crime Library Titles
by Gary C. King

THE TEXAS 7
AN EARLY GRAVE
MURDER IN HOLLYWOOD

MURDER IN HOLLYWOOD

GARY C. KING

St. Martin's Paperbacks

MURDER IN HOLLYWOOD

Copyright © 2001 by Gary C. King Enterprises, Inc.

Cover photographs courtesy AP/Wide World Photos.

ISBN: 0-312-98276-3

Printed in the United States of America

St. Martin's Paperbacks edition / August 2001

10 9 8 7 6 5 4 3 2 1

For Teresita,
with all of my love.

Acknowledgments

I GRATEFULLY ACKNOWLEDGE THE FOLLOWING PEO-
ple, without whose assistance this project would not
have been possible:

Peter Miller, my manager at PMA Literary and Film
Management, and his development associate, Kate
Garrick, both of whom assisted me every step of the
way and helped keep me focused during the often gru-
eling process of writing this book.

Charles E. Spicer Jr., Executive Editor at St. Martin's True Crime Library, for having the confidence in
me to do this project; Joe Cleemann, Associate Editor,
for his usual fine work editing the manuscript; Ander-
son Bailey for a superb job of finding and selecting the
photos for the insert and for helping to answer my
many questions; John Karle, publicity director, for arranging my interviews and appearances; and everyone
else at St. Martin's who helped bring this project to
fruition.

Thanks also to Marvin Wolf and Rift Fournier in
Los Angeles, and Steve Rosenthal in New York, for
your assistance.

A special acknowledgment for my Internet pals at
the True Crime Club and Trialwatchers.com for your
friendship and support, and for alerting me to late-
breaking news reports.

I am also deeply indebted to Bonnie Tiegel in Hol-

lywood and Don Jacobs and his crew in Las Vegas, of
Entertainment Tonight, and Leeza Gibbons and Harry
and his crew of *Extra.* I greatly appreciate all of the
kindness and professionalism that was shown me in
helping me promote this book.

And, as always, a very special thank you to Sarah
and Kirsten for your endless beautiful smiles and pa-
tience in putting up with your grouchy old pops during
the arduous and demanding schedule that was necessary to complete this project. I couldn't have done it
without you. I love you!

And where the offence is let the great axe fall.

WILLIAM SHAKESPEARE
Hamlet

Author's Note

THE STORY THAT FOLLOWS BROKE ON FRIDAY NIGHT, May 4, 2001, and continues to unfold as I write these words. Six weeks have passed since actor Robert Blake's wife, Bonny Lee Bakley, was murdered in Hollywood, California. The teams of detectives from the Los Angeles Police Department are still trying to figure out who killed her. This book makes no assumptions or presumptions regarding who Bonny's murderer might be—I simply do not know, and the LAPD has released few details. What I have attempted to do here is to present the facts of the case as they are known and as they have been presented to the public in various media formats—newspapers, magazines, tabloids, television and radio news and entertainment programs, and so forth. I have also refrained from making any judgments about Bonny's chosen lifestyle and her relationship with Blake, having decided that it is best that the reader make up his or her own mind after reading what is known. At this time there is no ending, at least not in the traditional sense of the word, because of all of the loose ends that still need to be tied up. This book marks the first time in the twenty years that I have been writing true crime that I have written about a case that has not reached a satisfying conclusion. But, if I may be so bold as to borrow a phrase, *the truth is out there!*

However, whether we ever find out just what the truth is remains to be seen.

The dialogue that appears herein is based on statements that were made in the news media as well as from my own interviews with certain individuals. The dialogue quoted from news sources includes but is not limited to the following: *The Los Angeles Times; The San Diego Union-Tribune; The San Francisco Chronicle; The New York Daily News; The New York Post;* The Associated Press; CNN; MSNBC; ABC News; CBS News; and *The National Enquirer.*

—G. C. K.
June 15, 2001

INTRODUCTION

"DON'T DO THE CRIME, IF YOU CAN'T DO THE TIME."

Those were the often-heard words of actor Robert Blake's tough-talking TV persona, Tony Baretta, the title character of the very popular series that ran on ABC from January 1975 to May 1978, and were echoed in the show's theme song. Baretta was a cop who lived in apartment 2-C of the seedy and run down King Edward Hotel with his talking pet cockatoo, Fred. *Baretta* probably could have gone far beyond its eighty episodes if not for Blake's off-camera battles with producers and screenwriters and his outlandish on-set behavior, purportedly caused by his alcohol and drug cravings that appeared to stem, at least in part, from a bad childhood. After *Baretta* finished its successful run, the former *Our Gang* child actor, who won critical acclaim as real-life killer Perry Smith in the 1967 film adaptation of Truman Capote's *In Cold Blood* (the second best selling true crime book of all time behind only Vincent Bugliosi's *Helter Skelter*), Blake, according to those who knew him, decided to opt out of show business. However, Blake was not absent from the Hollywood scene for long. Apparently able to get work when he wanted it, Blake soon returned to the small screen in 1985 as a priest, Father Noah "Hardstep" Rivers, in the television series, *Hell Town*. *Hell Town* was short-lived, however, and went off the air after 16 episodes, again by Blake's own choice. Blake went through a number of acting jobs throughout the 1980s and 1990s, but he shined in the 1993 CBS television movie, *Judgment Day: The John List Story*, which chronicles the true story of a man who killed his family. Blake received an Emmy nomination.

Now Blake is being investigated for the murder of his wife, Bonny Lee Bakley, in what has many of the ingredients to make Hollywood's next "O. J." case.

Bakley, a known con artist, grifter, star-chaser, porn peddler and wannabe movie star with a much checkered past, was known to have pursued celebrities such as Jerry Lee "The Killer" Lewis, Frankie Valli, Dean Martin, Christian Brando, Gary Busey, and others, prompting some people to characterize her as the having been somewhat like the Kate Hudson character in the movie, *Almost Famous*. Unable to break into the business, Bonny resigned herself to the notion that if she couldn't be a movie star, she would marry one. It was in that vein that she set a plan into motion to meet Robert Blake at a Los Angeles jazz club in 1999. After that, they became romantically involved and Bonny became pregnant. At first, after the baby girl was born in June 2000, she decided to name the child after Christian Brando, with whom she claimed to have slept. Later, at Blake's insistence, DNA tests were performed that confirmed Blake, not Brando, was the child's father. The revelation, along with discoveries about Bonny's past, marked Robert Blake's entry into a marriage from hell.

Before delving into the story that you are about to

read, a short history of Tinseltown and some of the murders and mysterious deaths that have occurred there over the years seems in order, to set the stage, so to speak, for the story that follows.

Hollywood, California, the motion picture capital of the world, sits in the basin of the San Fernando Valley, one of 24 named communities in the incorporated City of Los Angeles. Originally inhabited by Native Americans, Spanish settlement in the 1800s forced the Indians into the nearby missions of San Fernando and San Gabriel. The land that became the Hollywood area was divided into two Spanish land grants, the Rancho La Brea and the Rancho Los Feliz, which became primarily agricultural and provided crops such as bananas, pineapple, and a variety of citrus fruits. It wasn't until 1886 when H. H. Wilcox purchased a large portion of the Rancho La Brea that the area was named Hollywood, a name chosen by Wilcox's wife, Daeida.

The community grew quickly. Wealthy Midwesterners were looking for a suitable place to build their palatial winter homes—in Victorian, Queen Anne and Mission Revival architectural styles and Hollywood fit the bill. Churches went up, as did schools, a library, as well as a host of other businesses. Hollywood prospered and was incorporated in 1903. However, due to the lack of water, the community was annexed to the City of Los Angeles in 1910, which had been incorporated to pool resources for the construction of aqueducts.

The following year the Nestor Company opened

the city's first motion picture studio, near Sunset and
Gower. A short time later Cecil B. DeMille made history by producing the city's first feature film. D. W.
Griffith and Mack Sennett followed suit and opened
studios in the area that is now known as Echo Park,
and Hollywood began its transformation from an agricultural community to one of big business. Banking
and real estate soon moved in, and during the 1920s
and 1930s restaurants, grand movie theaters, and night
clubs popped up along Sunset Boulevard. Stretching
some 25 miles East to West and ending at the Pacific
Ocean, it quickly became known as the Sunset Strip.

Over the next two decades additional movie studios
came to town, and the celebrities in the film industry
moved into Beverly Hills, the Hollywood Hills, and
up the coast to Malibu. Music recording studios
moved into the area during the 1950s and 1960s along
Hollywood Boulevard and Sunset Boulevard, bringing
with them high-rise buildings constructed in Art Deco
and Modern styles. Nowadays on any given day or
night, prostitutes, pimps, street gangs, drug addicts,
and a host of other derelicts can be spotted just about
anywhere along Sunset and Hollywood Boulevards.
Although much of the glamour and elegance of yes-
teryear are now nearly nonexistent, the movie industry
remains and continues to pump out blockbusters
alongside its share of box office bombs.

Murder, like everywhere else, has not been a
stranger to Hollywood.

Over the past century, Hollywood has seen a great
deal of solved and unsolved homicides—some involving the famous, others of which involved the not

so famous. Many a tragedy, like the one detailed in this book, has been played out in this make-believe town that was built on dreams and failures.

One such homicide involved that of young and promiscuous aspiring actress, Virginia Rappe. She was a beautiful 26-year-old brunette model from Chicago who was known to sleep around with just about anyone who was somebody in Hollywood in order to make her dreams come true. Among those she was sleeping with was movie mogul Mack Sennett, which afforded Sennett's top comedian, Rosco "Fatty" Arbuckle, the opportunity to lust after Sennett's new plaything. It was no secret that Arbuckle wanted Virginia in the worst way, and he was determined to have his way with her or else.

Arbuckle had just signed a $3 million contract with Paramount, and he decided to throw a lavish party up the coast in San Francisco over Labor Day weekend, 1921. Arbuckle and his troupe checked into several suites on the twelfth floor of the St. Francis Hotel, and the party began early on Monday, September 5. Although Prohibition was in effect, the liquor flowed freely. At about 3 P.M. that day, Arbuckle brought Virginia, drunk on gin, to his room and was heard to say, "I've waited for this for a long time." Moments later terrifying, bloodcurdling screams were heard coming from Arbuckle's suite. When revelers barged into the room, they saw Virginia, naked and drenched with blood, convulsing in pain, moaning, "I'm dying . . . he hurt me." She died three days later of peritonitis caused by a ruptured bladder.

Forensic pathologists stated that Virginia had been

repeatedly raped with a large foreign object. Some speculated that she had been torn open by a soda pop bottle, while tabloids reported that Arbuckle had shoved a jagged piece of ice into her vagina. Arbuckle's story was that he found Virginia vomiting in his bathroom and helped clean her up before placing her on his bed. He claimed that he left her there to rejoin his party, only to return a few minutes later to find her in her bloody condition on the floor. But, like so many murder suspects, his story just didn't wash and he was eventually charged with rape and manslaughter in connection with her death.

Following two trials that ended in hung juries, Arbuckle was acquitted of Virginia Rappe's death in a third. His movie career, however, was all but over. Paramount cancelled his $3 million contract, and movie theaters around the country stopped playing his movies. In large part because of the Arbuckle-Rappe scandal, Hollywood created a self-policing organization known as the "Hays Office," with one Will Hays the president. In April 1922, Hays banned Arbuckle from film making, but lifted the ban later that same year. Nonetheless, Arbuckle's career was destroyed. He began drinking heavily and, never able to make a comeback, he died virtually broke. A fatal heart attack in his sleep ended his life on on June 29, 1933. He was 46.

The mysterious death of sex-pot Thelma Todd, 29, dubbed "The Ice Cream Blonde," on December 16, 1935, still haunts Hollywood to this day. Todd, who lived with her director and lover Roland West in a mansion between Malibu and Santa Monica, was found by her maid, slumped over the steering wheel of her Packard convertible in the garage. The night she died, Todd and West fought viciously and the fight ended only after West locked her out of the house. Neighbors reported hearing Todd shouting and cursing at West as she pounded on the mansion's front door. Nonetheless, a grand jury found that Todd's death was the result of "carbon monoxide poisoning," and it was generally believed that she arrived home intoxicated and fell asleep in the garage while her car's engine was running.

News reports and tabloids speculated at that time that West had become enraged with Thelma when he learned that she had gone out partying against his wishes, and when he found her inside the car with the engine running he closed the garage door and went to bed. West was never charged in Todd's death, and her death remains a mystery to this day.

Another murder that continues to fascinate Americans and remains unsolved is that of aspiring actress Elizabeth Short, 22, dubbed "The Black Dahlia," whose mutilated nude corpse was found lying in a vacant lot near Thirty-ninth Street and Coliseum on January 15, 1947. It is generally believed that Short was given the moniker of The Black Dahlia because of her raven black hair and the fact that she preferred to dress in black attire, although the precise source of the name remains as evasive as the person who killed her.

Short's gruesomely dismembered body was first seen by a passerby, who reported his grisly find to the police. Her body had been completely cut in half, and extensive bruising showed that she had been severely beaten. Grass had been shoved into her vagina, she had been sodomized after death, and the letters "BD" were rumored to have been carved into the flesh of one of her thighs. Her mouth had been viciously extended by horizontal cuts, and portions of her lips had been surgically removed. Portions of flesh also had been cut away from her upper and lower torso. Short's murder was without question one of the more gruesome murders that Hollywood has seen and, while still on the books, police are no closer to solving it now than they were in 1947.

In 1958 actress Lana Turner, considered a sex goddess at the time, was an Oscar nominee for her performance in 1957's *Peyton Place*. Turner had been fooling around with underworld figure Johnny Stompanato, a handsome smooth talker who had served as a chauffeur and bagman for Los Angeles gangster Mickey Cohen (himself known for picking up wealthy married women and surreptitiously filming his lovemaking sessions with them so that he could extort staggering figures afterward by "selling" the films to them).

Turner's relationship with Stompanato was stormy, and he was known to regularly beat her. On one occasion, after she turned him down for a $50,000 loan he needed to secure the script rights for a movie in which he wanted to star, Stompanato stormed onto the set where she was rehearsing, *Another Time, Another Place* with Sean Connery. He warned Connery to stay away from Turner, waving a gun in the Scotsman's face. Connery, not taken kindly to being threatened, reportedly punched his lights out.

It wasn't long after that incident that Turner ordered Stomanato to move out of her townhouse. Stompanato went into a rage saying, "I'll mutilate you! I'll hurt you so that you'll be so repulsive you'll have to hide forever!" Hearing the commotion, Turner's only child, 14-year-old Cheryl Crane, entered the room and witnessed Stompanato choking her mother in the bedroom and threatening to "cut her" with a razor. Fearing for her mother's life, Cheryl ran to the kitchen and grabbed a knife that she plunged into Stompanato's stomach upon her return. Stompanato died from the injury. However, a coroner's jury ruled that Cheryl Crane had committed justifiable homicide. While there was very little mystery to the case, many people considered Stompanato a scumbag who deserved what he got and the sensational case is still talked about to this day.

There hasn't been a decade in recent memory in which a sensational murder did not occur in Hollywood. As the 1960s were winding down, with Richard M. Nixon barely seven months into his presidency and the Vietnam War still going strong, the City of Angels bore witness to two occurrences of senseless, wholesale slaughter that will not easily be forgotten.

Charles Manson, 34, illegitimate son of a teenage prostitute, had spent most of his teenage and adult life in prisons for a variety of crimes, ranging from car theft to taking underage females across state lines for immoral purposes, i.e. pimping them out as prostitutes. An avowed racist after being raped by black men in prison, with a deep-seated hatred for authority,

Manson was little more than an acidhead nutcase bent on forming a cult of misguided female followers that he would persuade to do his bidding for him. After gathering up a group of washed-out women and a few equally down and out men, Manson moved his "family" onto the dilapidated Spahn Movie Ranch in eastern Simi Valley. He took on the persona of Son of Man (taken from the two syllables of his name, Man-Son) and preached gibberish to his newfound followers. Having written an idiotic two-word song titled, "You Know," Manson, fancied himself a musician and relentlessly tried to get the song published, to no avail. At one point, he had approached actress Doris Day's son, Terry Melcher, who had connections with people in the music industry. Melcher brushed him off, however, angering the diminutive five feet two inch Manson. He vowed to exact revenge and show Melcher that he meant business.

A few months before the slaughter occurred, Manson and one of his cohorts, Charles "Tex" Watson, 23, went to Melcher's sprawling estate on Cielo Drive in Benedict Canyon, presumably to kill him, only to find that Melcher no longer lived there. Instead they viewed a number of people coming and going, people they figured were movie stars, and it was then that Manson got the idea that he would have everyone who lived there killed to teach Melcher a lesson and to terrify him into promoting Manson's musical masterpiece.

Manson's followers, sans Manson himself, converged on the Cielo Drive home on the night of August 8, 1969. Eight-month-pregnant Sharon Tate, the beautiful, blonde movie star and wife of film director Roman Polanski, was inside. With her were coffee heiress Abigail Folger and her boyfriend, writer Voyteck Frykowski, a friend of Polanski's. Celebrated hair stylist to the rich and famous, Jay Sebring, a former boyfriend of Tate's, was also there. Manson's instructions to Tex Watson, Patricia Krenwinkel, 21, Susan Atkins, 21, and Linda Kasabian, 20, were to kill everyone inside the house and to make the killings "as gruesome as possible." Armed with a knife, a.22-caliber revolver, and rope, they followed their leader's instructions.

When they entered the grounds they encountered Steven Parent, 18, who had been visiting the caretaker. As Parent pleaded and begged for his life, Watson shot him four times, killing him almost instantly. Once inside the house they rounded up Tate, Sebring, Frykowski and Folger, and took them into the living room. They tied up Sebring and assured the terrified victims that they were only there to commit a robbery and would do them no harm.

Sebring, however, freed himself and attempted to flee but was shot to death in the process. Frykowski, sensing that they would all meet the same fate if they didn't do something, attempted to bolt. However, he was shot, too, and while writhing in pain on the floor he was kicked and beaten while the females in the group stabbed him a total of 51 times. When Abigail Folger attempted to make a break for it through the back door, Krenwinkel knocked her down in the yard and Watson stabbed her to death. Sharon Tate was the last to be killed, stabbed 16 times as she begged for her unborn child's life. They wrote the word "pig" in Tate's blood on the home's front door.

Manson's bloody rampage wasn't finished, however. Two nights later, on August 10, Manson ordered Watson, Krenwinkel, and Leslie Van Houten, 19, to enter the randomly selected home of Leno and Rosemary LaBianca and to murder the inhabitants. Watson stabbed Leno repeatedly on the living room floor and left the knife sticking in his neck while Krenwinkel and Van Houten stabbed Rosemary 41 times in another room. They wrote "Death to all pigs" and "Rise" in their victims' blood on a living room wall, and the words "Healter (sic) Skelter" on the refrigerator door. Afterward they took a shower together to wash away all the blood. Before leaving Watson took a knife from the kitchen and carved the word "War" on Leno LaBianca's stomach. As a final touch he thrust the knife into the victim's stomach. Manson and his gang were eventually apprehended and sentenced to die in California's gas chamber. However, when the death penalty was abolished for a number of years beginning in 1972, their sentences were commuted to life in prison.

The 1970s saw the murder of 37-year-old actor and Oscar nominee Sal Mineo, who had been somewhat well-known for the films he made when he was younger. Mineo dropped out of show business despite his early success, either of his own volition or because it became more and more difficult for him to find work. On February 13, 1976, while he was returning to his apartment near Sunset Boulevard, a career criminal named Lionel Williams lay in wait in the carport, armed with a hunting knife. Williams, who had a history of robbing apartments in Hollywood, stabbed Mineo several times in the chest as the actor prepared to enter his unit. As Williams prepared to steal Mineo's wallet, a neighbor came out and frightened him away. Mineo was dead within minutes from massive hemorrhaging.

Days later, while Williams was sitting in jail after an arrest for robbery, he made comments that Sal Mineo had been killed because of drugs. The police paid him little mind, however, because they had found no evidence that Mineo used or was otherwise involved in drugs. A year passed, and while Williams was doing time in Michigan for writing bad checks, his wife went to the police in Los Angeles and told detectives that her husband had killed Mineo. She explained that he had told her on the night of the murder that he had done it with a hunting knife. She described the knife to the police, and the coroner determined that the type of knife she had described would match the stab wounds in Mineo's chest.

Although Williams had bragged to jailers in Michigan about the murder, no one seemed to believe him at the time and it took until January 1979 for him to be returned to California to stand trial. He was found guilty of Mineo's murder, and for 10 robberies in Hollywood, and was sentenced to fifty-one years to life in prison.

In the 1980s, beautiful 18-year-old Dorothy Ruth Hoogstraten was "discovered" by a pimp named Paul

Snider. Snider had met Dorothy three years earlier at
a Vancouver, British Columbia, Dairy Queen where
she worked as a cashier. Snider promised her the
world, telling her she could be Playmate of the Year
for *Playboy* magazine. With few ambitions, Dorothy
fell for Snider's promises, and together they moved
to Hollywood. She changed her name to Dorothy
Stratten.

Although she didn't make Playmate of the Year the
first time around, she was selected as the magazine's
August 1979 Playmate of the Month. Snider and Stratten were married, and Snider actively sought film
roles for his new wife who had a natural talent for
acting. She obtained a few small roles as a result of
Snider's efforts, and in 1980 *Playboy* did in fact name
her Playmate of the Year. Afterward, more doors were
opened as producers and major studios began to take
her more seriously.

It wasn't long before Dorothy began seeing other
men in the business, and at one point she went to New
York to appear in a Peter Bogdanovich film. During
production she and Bogdanovich began an affair, and
when she returned to Hollywood she dumped Snider
for the director. On August 14, 1980, Dorothy showed
up at Snider's home in a prearranged meeting to go
over the final details of the divorce. She didn't leave,
alive. Snider killed her with a shotgun, then turned
the gun on himself.

The 1980s also saw the brutal and senseless murder
of 21-year-old actress Rebecca Schaeffer, who was
co-starring in a television series with Pam Dawber
called *My Sister Sam*. Rebecca had a fan, an admirer

with a dark side, who had been stalking her for some time. Infatuated with the lovely actress after her public relations people had sent him a photograph of her, Robert John Bardo, had obtained her address by paying a private detective firm $250 to check California's motor vehicle division's files. Once he had her address in hand, Bardo decided to pay Rebecca a visit.

Rebecca was at home on the morning of July 18, 1989, reading a new batch of recently delivered scripts. She was unaware that Bardo was outside her building pacing up and down the street, and had been doing so since before dawn. He finally worked up enough nerve to walk up and ring the bell to her apartment. When she answered the door, Bardo reached into his pocket and pulled out a photograph of her.

"You sent this to me," Bardo told Schaeffer. "I'm your biggest fan. I just want to talk to you."

"I'm busy," Rebecca replied. "Please go away. I don't have time right now."

Bardo went back toward the street, but he was very upset with his favorite actress. A short time later he went back into the building and rang the bell to her apartment again. When she answered the door, Bardo shot her in the chest at point blank range. Rebecca died almost instantly, and Bardo was eventually convicted of her murder and sentenced to life in prison.

There were others, of course, like the unsolved murder of actor William Desmond Taylor in 1922, the questionable death of actor John Garfield in 1952, the mysterious "suicide" of Marilyn Monroe in 1962, and the chilling murder of *Poltergeist* actress Dominique

Dunne in 1981. And who could forget the June 1994 murders of Nicole Brown Simpson and Ron Goldman—what a way to round out Hollywood's final years of the century! Hollywood murders, however, like that of Bonny Lee Bakley, whose death is as senseless and mysterious as many of the murders that came before hers, get considerably more attention than murders that occur elsewhere. The glitz and the glamorous façade of the motion picture capital of the world, and the celebrities who are sometimes involved make Hollywood murders the most closely followed murders.

So who killed Bonny Lee Bakley, you're probably asking? The Los Angeles Police Department claims that it does not have enough evidence to arrest anyone at this point. Blake has secured the services of two highly skilled and competent criminal defense attorneys. Blake's lawyers say their client didn't do it; Bakley's relatives, however, have publicly stated that Bonny had expressed fear for her life and told family members shortly before her death that if anything ever happened to her, Blake was behind it. Despite being under intense public scrutiny, the LAPD isn't talking. With the reputation of the LAPD once again hanging in the balance after Rodney King, O. J. Simpson, and the Ramparts Division scandal, Captain James Tatreau of the LAPD Robbery–Homicide Bureau is demanding that every procedure be conducted with flawless precision right down to dotting every "i" and crossing every "t." When an arrest is made, no questions will arise regarding the integrity of the LAPD and their investigation of this case.

Whoever killed Bonny, the burning question remains in everyone's minds: why would anyone gun down in cold blood this mother of an infant girl? But here's the story of her murder, her life of scamming men, her star stalking, and her relationship with Robert Blake, one of the most eccentric celebrities in Hollywood. Here also is the story of how he is being investigated by the police and the media in connection with his wife's death.

CHAPTER 1

STUDIO CITY, CALIFORNIA, LOCATED ON THE NORTH-
ern foothills of the Santa Monica mountains, was
named in part because of the movies and short features that were being made by Mack Sennett during
the 1920s silent era. The Central Motion Picture District put up $20 million for a film alliance, that was
aptly named Studio City. Sennett then began shooting
short two-reel films such as *The Keystone Cops.* In
1935 Republic Pictures basically took over the area,
and attracted such stars as Bette Davis, Ronald Rea-
gan, Tony Curtis, James Stewart, Ray Milland, Jack
Webb, John Wayne, Errol Flynn, and Roy Rogers, to
name only a few. Even Alfred Hitchcock made his
claim to fame at Republic during this time frame. Located some 15 miles from downtown Los Angeles,
Studio City provided quick and easy access to Hollywood and Beverly Hills. The city soon had a reputation for being a safe place to live and a great place
to raise children. The economy prospered over the
years as businesses such as boutiques, banks, and fine
restaurants popped up along Ventura Boulevard and
elsewhere. By the mid-1980s, CBS and MTM Studios
were producing such hits as *Newhart, Thirtysome-
thing,* and *Roseanne* there, and even today, in the new
millennium, with a population of only about 30,000
people, Studio City is considered one of the most de-

sirable places to live within the City of Los Angeles and is often referred to as the Jewel of the Valley, a name it has kept since its beginnings. However, it has not been without its problems, including violent crime.

It was during the cool early evening hours of Friday, May 4, 2001 that actor Robert Blake, 67, a Hollywood carryover from those earlier years, and Bonny Lee Bakley, 44, his wife, parked their 1991 black Dodge Stealth on the south side of Woodbridge Street. The car faced east and sat beneath a burned-out street lamp and a few feet behind a Dumpster.

They strolled arm-in-arm a block and a half to Vitello's Italian Restaurant, located at 4349 Tujunga Avenue. It was a nice, clear evening, even if, at 60 degrees, a bit on the chilly side for Southern California. A slight breeze would have hit them on the short walk from the car to the restaurant.

Vitello's is a large, highly rated family-owned restaurant with a casual Mediterranean ambiance and fresco-painted walls, freshly baked bread, and some of the best Italian food in the San Fernando Valley. Reservations are rarely needed, and it was one of Blake's favorite restaurants. He was known to eat there frequently, often two or three times a week over the last 20 years, enough for the owners to name a tomato and spinach pasta dish after him, *fusilli à la Robert Blake*. On that particular evening, Blake and Bonny were there to discuss their future plans and their somewhat troubled relationship. Blake's grown daughter, Delinah, cared for their 11-month-old daughter, Rose, at her home in Hidden Hills.

After they entered Vitello's, Joseph Restivo, who co-owns the restaurant with his brother, Steve Restivo, seated the couple, not at Blake's usual corner booth, number 42, but at a booth near the rear of the restaurant that was still visible to the other dining patrons. Both Blake and his wife dined, Blake having his tomato and spinach pasta dish, and they enjoyed the restaurant pianist as he played Blake's favorite song, "I Remember You."

Halfway through dinner, however, while Bonny was drinking her third glass of red wine, Blake excused himself and went to the men's room where another patron reportedly witnessed him vomiting into a trash can, pulling at his hair, and mumbling to himself. When Blake walked out of the men's room, he appeared somewhat agitated, shaky and ill, according to the patron who saw him vomit. Blake did not drink any alcohol that evening, and he did not complain to his waiter or to the owners about the food. He simply returned to his booth, paid with a credit card, left their waiter a 25 percent tip, and exited the establishment sometime between 9:30 and 9:40 P.M. Together, he and Bonny walked back to the black Stealth. After letting Bonny into the car, Blake realized that he had left a handgun at the restaurant. (He had begun carrying it recently because of Bonny's fear for her safety.) He told her that he would be right back and purportedly walked back to Vitello's to retrieve it.

When he returned to the car minutes later he found Bonny slumped over in the passenger seat, unconscious and bleeding from a wound to her head. Unable to revive her, Blake ran to the home of filmmaker

Sean Stanek, located directly behind Vitello's and just across the street from the car. This marked the beginning of a case that would rock Hollywood like it hadn't been rocked since O. J. Simpson was accused of killing his wife, Nicole, and her friend, Ronald Goldman.

Shaking and vomiting, Blake pounded repeatedly on Stanek's front door and rang his doorbell until the filmmaker opened it. He recognized Robert Blake, dressed completely in black and wearing a black cap, having seen him frequently in cafés and restaurants in the neighborhood, including Vitello's. At first Stanek thought that someone was playing a prank on him, but when he saw the anguish and terror in Blake's face he knew something was terribly wrong.

"She's hurt! I need help!" yelled Blake in a highly agitated state. "Dear God, someone please help me!" As Stanek tried to calm him down, the actor, crying and shaking, told Stanek that his wife had been hurt and asked him to call 911, which Stanek did. Afterward, they ran across the street to Blake's car. By then it was 9:50 P.M.

When they got to the car, Stanek took over while Blake claimed that he ran back to Vitello's to try and seek medical help, to see if there was a doctor or a nurse inside the restaurant. A nurse reportedly got up from her table and accompanied Blake outside to see if there was anything she could do to help, but Blake did not return to the car to check on his wife's condition.

While Blake was away, Stanek noted that the car's passenger window was rolled down, and there was no sign of shattered glass. The inside of the car was covered with blood. Bonny, however, was still alive. She was making gurgling sounds and was gasping for air, and her eyes were rolling backward. Stanek listened intently on his cellular phone as he received first-aid instructions from a 911 operator who told him to try and stop the bleeding by pressing a towel against the wound on her head. Cradling her head in his arms, covering the wound with a towel that was fast becoming blood-soaked, Stanek could see that she was still breathing. But his efforts to save her appeared hopeless. He began speaking to her in an attempt to elicit a response from the gravely injured woman.

"Can you hear my voice?" Stanek asked. "If you can hear me, please squeeze my hand." However, there was no response.

Paramedics arrived at the scene seven minutes after receiving the 911 call from Stanek. They took over and performed CPR in an attempt to revive her, to no avail. Blake did not go near his wife while the paramedics were treating her, possibly because he did not want to interfere with their work. After treating her as best they could at the scene, the paramedics loaded her onto an ambulance and sped to a nearby hospital ten minutes later. However, despite everyone's best efforts to save her, Bonny Lee Bakley was declared dead on arrival at St. Joseph's Medical Center in Burbank.

When the police arrived, Blake was sitting on the street curb, crying and vomiting. A policeman sat down and put his arm around him in an attempt to console him. When Blake was composed enough to provide a statement, he told the police officers that he and his wife, whom he identified as Leebonny Bakely, had dined at Vitello's. When they had gotten back to the car, he said, he realized that he had forgotten something, a handgun licensed to him and that he carried because Bonny feared that she was being stalked. He said that the weapon had apparently slipped out of his waistband and onto the seat of the booth that they had occupied. He had gone back to the restaurant to retrieve it. When he returned to the car, he found that his wife had been shot once behind the right ear and once in the shoulder. That was when he ran to Stanek's home to call the police, according to LAPD spokesman Guillermo Campos.

Blake declined to take a polygraph test that evening, contending that he was much too distraught. Blake also purportedly said that he feared that he would fail the test because, as in the O. J. Simpson case, he had dreams of killing her and that alone might cause him to fail the test. He also reportedly said that he blamed himself for her death for leaving her alone in the car.

"He was falling apart," Stanek said. "He was incoherently in shock, guttural agony cries . . . he was sick. He was throwing up. He was shaken up. He was crying . . . he was really messed up."

The shooting that had occurred on Woodbridge Street that night was totally out of character for this San Fernando Valley neighborhood comprised of mostly modest older homes, some of which have been remodeled or are in the process of being remodeled. It had always been a quiet neighborhood.

"This is the most peaceful, beautiful neighborhood," said a resident of Woodbridge Street who came out to see what all of the police and paramedic activities were about. "This is not the type of neighborhood where things like this happen."

When police detectives arrived on the scene they interviewed Blake about the evening's events in an interview that took some five hours to complete. The police released few details afterward, and stressed that they had interviewed Blake only as a witness to a homicide and not as a suspect. They worked throughout the night and into the next day trying to put the pieces to this most unusual homicide puzzle together.

Among the people that investigators talked to in the hours after the slaying were neighborhood residents Andrew Percival and his wife, who had been dining at Vitello's on Friday evening during the same time frame that Blake and Bonny had been there. Percival, who said that he and his wife had left the restaurant at about 9:30 P.M., told the investigators that he had seen a man dressed in black and who looked like Blake inside the restaurant. After Percival and his wife paid their bill and began walking toward their home, located nearby, they saw the same man dressed in black walking "very, very briskly" past them in the middle of the street and toward the car parked behind the Dumpster. Percival remarked that crime was uncommon in the neighborhood.

"This is a really nice neighborhood," Percival said. "Crime just isn't an issue around here."

As they pressed on with their inquiry the investigators spoke with Vitello's co-owner, Joseph Restivo, and found what appeared to be a major hole in Blake's account of the evening's activities. Blake had initially told the police that he had returned to Vitello's once to retrieve the gun, and then went back to the restaurant again to seek medical assistance for his gravely wounded wife. However, according to what Restivo told investigators, Blake only returned to the restaurant one time, apparently following the shooting.

"He ran in here saying something had happened," Restivo said. "He asked for a glass of water. He first said his wife had been hurt, then he said she had fallen down. Finally he said she had been shot . . . he was saying that she had been mugged or got shot and asked me to call 911." Before Restivo could complete the call, Blake told him it wasn't necessary. " 'It's okay, it's already done,' " Restivo quoted Blake as having said. "He asked for water, drank it here, and left . . . the guy was nuts." Blake reportedly drank two glasses of water while inside the restaurant.

Steve Restivo, who owns Vitello's along with Joseph, left the restaurant for the evening before Blake and his wife. He later told investigators that Blake and Bonny seemed happy and relaxed that evening. Having seen Blake sipping his soup, chicken broth without vegetables, directly from the bowl, Restivo said that he quipped that Blake appeared more Sicilian than his own father, to which Blake responded that the soup had helped keep him from catching the flu all winter.

The investigators learned from conducting interviews with restaurant employees that Blake's table was bussed within two minutes of his departure, but no gun had been found there. Furthermore, there were no employees or customers who saw him return to the restaurant at the time the shooting was believed to have occurred. Witnesses only remembered seeing him at the establishment after the shooting when he came in asking for help and drank the two glasses of water.

Because the spouse of a murder victim or the last person to see a victim alive is nearly always placed at the top of the suspect list Blake would, naturally, be looked at closely. The apparent incoherence in Blake's account of the events of that evening only served to make him even more of a suspect in his wife's death. But before the investigators could draw any conclusions about the identity of Bonny's killer they knew that there was much more to be looked at in this case. Blake, for example, would have to undergo gunshot-residue testing to determine if there were traces of gunpowder on his hands and clothing. That would establish, hopefully, whether or not he had fired a gun recently.

Another potentially troubling aspect of the case was the fact that Blake had been coming to Vitello's for 20 years without making reservations. Vitello's normally did not require reservations, but on the evening of May 4, Blake made a reservation for the first time. He was also known to use the restaurant's valet parking service, which he did not utilize that night, instead choosing to park a block and a half away and walk to the restaurant with his wife. He also introduced Bonny as his wife to the staff that evening, even though he had brought her to the restaurant on prior occasions. No one at the restaurant recalled knowing that Blake was even married.

What did it all mean? Nothing at this point. These were just some among many interesting facts that further served to place a cloud of doubt over Blake's situation. The police knew that much more than circumstantial evidence would be needed if they were going to make a case against Blake. They would need hard physical evidence, scientific evidence, and, ideally, an eyewitness to the murder. There was much to be done before they could draw any conclusions about Blake, and they would soon learn that their investigation would take them in many different directions. They would learn in the coming days that any number of people out of Bonny's past might have wanted her dead, an eventuality that could ultimately shift their focus away from Blake, and rightly so. Just because Blake was her husband and was believed to have been the last person to have seen her alive didn't necessarily mean that he killed her. It was of paramount importance that all avenues be investigated to ensure that they nailed the right person.

Nobody, at this juncture, wanted to see *Baretta*, the TV cop hero, arrested for murder.

CHAPTER 2

IN THE MEANTIME, THE LOS ANGELES POLICE DE-partment, foreseeing the intense public scrutiny that this case would receive because a celebrity was being questioned, assigned its top detectives from the Robbery-Homicide Division to the investigation, a team of 16 investigators that would be led by Captain James Tatreau. Because of problems associated with the Rodney King case of the early 1990s, the O. J. Simpson case, and the more recent Ramparts Division Scandal, Los Angeles Police Chief Bernard Parks and the police commissioners were going to make certain that this case was handled methodically and by the book, with their every move made with the consultation of the district attorney's office. There could be no slipups or mistakes associated with this case.

On Saturday, May 5, 2001, the team of detectives from LAPD's Robbery-Homicide Division converged on Blake's rustic Mata Hari Ranch, on Dilling Street in Studio City, about five minutes from Vitello's. The brown, ranch-style home was in need of repair and a paint job, and included two carports added on at some point in the house's history. The longer of the two carports had an older model station wagon parked beneath it and the shorter one apparently was being used as a lounge area and was equipped with a cushioned swing and a lawn chair. An older-model van was parked on the grass, and lawn tools were propped up against the front of the house. An upside-down five-gallon bucket lay near the front door. A five-foot fence and gate covered in wire mesh, similar to chicken wire, enclosed the property. And Blake, a bird lover, kept an aviary outside his home.

The home and property did not have the character normally associated with a celebrity, but then, the detectives really didn't know Robert Blake. As they approached the house they could see from the driveway another white stucco home, a bungalow, behind the main residence. They were told the night before, when Blake allowed officers into the dwelling, that was where Bonny Bakley had lived. They walked to the front door of the main residence and knocked loudly.

When Blake came to the door they presented the actor with a warrant to search his home. They also conducted yet another interview with him about the previous evening's events. About an hour into the interview, the detectives purportedly accused him point-blank of murdering his wife. Blake, unable to throw the cops out of his home because of the search warrant, promptly stopped the interview. It was learned a short time later that Blake had hired high-profile criminal defense attorney Harland Braun, who had worked on the Rodney King police brutality case and the more recent and far-reaching LAPD Rampart Division investigation, which alleges police corruption and civil rights violations. Later that afternoon Blake came out of his home accompanied by three men as police officers, detectives, and reporters on the street looked on. Wearing a black baseball cap, a light blue T-shirt and sunglasses, Blake climbed into the passenger seat of a waiting Mercedes-Benz sedan and was driven away. An LAPD cruiser followed Blake and his entourage, whose destination was not revealed.

"He was not arrested," LAPD spokesman Guillermo Campos said. "He's as free as a bird."

In response to a pack of ravenous reporters representing several different news organizations, LAPD spokesman Don Hartwell announced that afternoon that Robert Blake was not a suspect in his wife's murder.

"He was interviewed like any witness would be interviewed, but he wasn't questioned," Hartwell said. "Mr. Blake realized that he had left some property in the restaurant and he went back to the establishment and retrieved the property. Upon his return to the vehicle, he discovered the injury to his wife . . . he was interviewed as a witness to the crime . . . there is no weapon that has been recovered at this point, and there are no primary suspects." However, Hartwell added when asked if his status could change: "Anything can change."

In the meantime, while one group of investigators removed several items from Blake's home and the house behind it where Bonny lived, another group of investigators returned to Vitello's and removed a large trash bin from the restaurant's parking lot. Similarly, an independent contractor was brought in to remove the Dumpster on Woodbridge Street. Blake had parked about six feet behind it on the night of the murder. The contractor was instructed to take it to a secure police location where its contents could be examined under more controlled surroundings. They didn't want to risk losing potential evidence to the elements of nature.

Blake returned to his rustic one-level dwelling on Dilling Street shortly after 8:30 P.M. Saturday. He was hunkered down in the seat of the same Mercedes-Benz that had earlier whisked him away, and this time he covered his face with his baseball cap in an attempt to avoid the members of the media that were camped outside his house. A man in the sedan's backseat got out and held up the yellow police tape so that the car could pass beneath it and park in the driveway. Approximately 30 minutes later the Mercedes, carrying Blake, left again. This time it was gone only a few minutes, and when it returned attorney Harland Braun got out and told reporters that Blake had been taken to a hospital for high blood pressure.

"He's in an absolute state of shock," Braun told reporters. "He's doing fine and has it under control. But the doctors want to keep him a little bit longer to make sure he's okay." Braun told reporters that Blake would likely remain in the hospital for a couple of days. However, he would be released from the hospital the following morning.

Braun stated that Bonny believed that someone had been stalking her in recent weeks and feared for her life. She had asked Blake to start carrying a gun. The gun, which Blake retrieved the night of the murder and turned over to the police, was licensed for Blake to carry by the Culver City Police Department and, according to Braun, Blake owned numerous guns that he kept inside his house. Braun also said that Bonny had an "interesting past . . . that may have caught up with her," but did not elaborate at that time beyond saying, "Apparently she's had some criminal history, so it could be any number of people that had it in for her."

Why had Blake parked his car a block and a half away from the restaurant, on a side street, when he could have used the restaurant's parking lot or valet parking? So no one would notice it, Braun said.

When asked why Blake would have left Bonny alone in the car to return to the restaurant to retrieve his gun, Braun told reporters that it had been a spur-of-the-moment decision.

"In hindsight," Braun said, "he wished he hadn't done that. But he just reacted instantly, having left the gun behind. And remember, there was not anything specific [about Bonny's fears for her life] . . . he just forgot it, like anyone who ever left behind an umbrella . . . he just knew that she had a generalized concern and maybe he thought she was a little paranoid."

According to Braun, Blake only married Bonny because he had gotten her pregnant. Their relationship began as a casual sexual relationship, and Blake, according to Braun, had felt that she had tricked him into marrying him by allowing herself to get pregnant.

"He married her out of a sense of obligation," Braun said. "They were not close . . . the nature of her business was to con people, especially those desperately in need and the lonely . . . It may have been some business associate [that killed her]. It could have been a relative . . . when you are dealing with people's emotions like that someone could come out and kill her.

"Murder is usually a highly motivated thing," Braun said, "but here we have a woman we don't know a lot about. Someone took that opportunity to kill her when Robert left the car. She was very vulnerable."

Braun said that despite the fact that Bonny occupied the house in back of Blake's, their marriage was improving.

"It wasn't your normal love," he said. "It wasn't a loving relationship. He married her because she's the mother of his daughter . . . they had a common interest in the child."

Blake's civil lawyer, Barry Felsen, who represented Blake in his business and entertainment affairs, echoed some of Braun's comments. According to Felsen, Blake and his wife had a difficult relationship and had become involved in an uneasy dispute over the child shortly after she was born on June 2, 2000. Because of a purported ongoing romantic relationship with Christian Brando, Marlon Brando's son, Bonny, thinking that the child was Christian's, named the girl Christian Shannon Brando. (Brando had spent five years of a ten-year sentence in prison after pleading guilty to voluntary manslaughter in the shooting death of his half sister Cheyenne's boyfriend, Dag Drollet). Most of the claims that she had been involved with Christian Brando had come from Bonny herself, and there remains a great deal of uncertainty surrounding the extent of the relationship. Nonetheless, at one point she told Blake that she wasn't sure if the child was Brando's or Blake's, prompting Blake to insist that DNA tests be performed. The test results proved Robert Blake was the girl's father. Afterward, Blake "did the right thing," according to Felsen, and married Bonny. Despite the fact that he married her, however, he hired private investigators to begin delving into her background.

Because of questions that had arisen about her past, Felsen said that a prenuptial agreement had been drawn up before she and Blake married on November 15, 2000, as well as an addendum to the prenuptial agreement that required her to refrain from committing illegal activities on Blake's property. The agreement didn't stop her, however, according to Felsen.

"She had trunks full of stuff," he said. "She was still placing classified ads in newspapers. I don't know if you would call it porn business, but she would send [men] nude photographs of herself, and they would send her money and she would promise to meet them."

Few people in Blake's neighborhood knew Bonny despite the fact that she and Blake had been married for nearly seven months at the time of her death. Most did not even know that the two were married.

"I never saw her," said a U.S. Postal Service employee who delivered mail to Blake's Dilling Street home. "He was a real nice guy and has a beautiful daughter."

Blake's neighbors, in the meantime, referred to the actor as a "nice man," but said that they did not know much about him or his wife.

"It's bizarre," said one of Blake's neighbors, referring to the murder and the investigation. "It's very bizarre. A little bit disconcerting, to say the least. But you know, hopefully it turns out to be just a bad set of circumstances."

After the search of Blake's home was completed, the LAPD remained tight-lipped about what was seized. They also refused to comment on a possible motive for Bonny's murder. However, it was leaked to the media that detectives had found the following words written on the bathroom walls of Blake's home: I'M NOT GOING DOWN FOR THIS.

CHAPTER 3

IN THE AFTERMATH OF BONNY LEE BAKLEY'S MUR-
der, initial reports began to surface regarding the results of Robert Blake's gunpowder-residue tests. Two
were administered, most likely a trace-metal detection
test and a neutron-activation analysis test. Interest-
ingly, it turned out that most of the reports circulating
about Blake's tests conflicted with each other despite
the fact that the LAPD steadfastly maintained that the
results had not come back yet. Nonetheless, some
published reports, possibly gleaned from information
leaked by someone within the LAPD, indicated that
the tests were inconclusive. Blake's attorney, Harland
Braun, on the other hand, contended that the test results had come back negative, while still other published reports contended that the results had been
positive. If traces of gunpowder residue had been
found on Blake it could have been because he had
been target practicing recently with the gun he was
carrying to protect his wife. At one point it was even
said that the FBI was studying the results of those
tests for the LAPD and that detectives were waiting
for the FBI's report.

The gunpowder residue tests might have no forensic value at all to the investigation. A trace-metal detection test can determine whether or not a person has
recently been in contact with metal. Big deal. In that

test, if Blake had touched any metal at all in the hours before the test was administered, the test results could come back positive, which would prove nothing other than that he had touched metal. He could have easily done that by opening the front gate at his house or by opening the car door for Bonny.

If a more specific type of test was administered, such as the one in which the investigators look for the presence of barium and antimony and which encompasses neutron activation analysis, a positive test result could indicate whether the person being examined was contaminated with "blow-back" residue from having recently fired a weapon. Such residues are typically removed from the subject by swabbing the back of the index finger, thumb and the web areas of the hand with a moistened cotton swab containing a solution of five percent nitric acid. But again, the value of such an examination is questionable since barium and antimony are found in nature, as well as in a variety of common products, and it was always possible that the subject being examined had come into contact with those elements from some action other than firing a gun. Most such tests are inconclusive because the individual who administers the test cannot state with an adequate degree of confidence that the subject fired a gun. Even when such test results come back positive, a suspect's defense lawyer can bring in other forensic experts who can challenge or dispute the original findings-based on different interpretations of the test results. Because of the ambiguity associated with such tests, a prosecutor's case can actually be damaged if the test results are not backed up with sufficient additional forensic evidence that points toward the suspect's guilt.

Meanwhile, the LAPD's investigation of Bonny Bakley's murder was strongly criticized by Blake's lawyer, Harland Braun. Braun stated that the investigators had not searched Bonny's residence thoroughly and had left behind several boxes of documents during their initial search that potentially could lead the police to a suspect. Instead, charged Braun, the investigation appeared to be focusing solely on Blake and singling out his client when there were others who should be looked at as possible suspects.

Braun indicated that Bonny Bakley was a schemer and a con artist, who solicited lonely men for money with a mail-order business in which she sold nude photos of herself. He hinted that much more would come out about her background as the investigation progressed, and suggested that whoever killed her was likely someone out of her past.

"It could be a business associate that hates her," Braun said. "It could be someone she took advantage of. If [Blake] didn't do it, it's someone from her past. And I don't think he did it . . . he's already given them five hours of interviews and they have taken routine tests from his clothing and his hands, which all came back negative."

"There has been much talk about who is or who is not a suspect," Captain James Tatreau responded. "We have not ruled anyone out as a suspect in this case . . . we're approaching the case as it should be investigated, following leads and conducting interviews. There is evidence that we will not be talking about, or the results of examination of that evidence."

It was noted that the clothing Blake had worn on the night of his wife's murder was seized by detectives and would undergo scientific testing, not only for the presence of gunpowder residue but likely also for blood-spatter analysis. It was also revealed that the Federal Bureau of Alcohol, Tobacco, and Firearms was conducting firearms examinations on one or more of Blake's handguns.

According to *The New York Daily News*, a highly placed source within the LAPD said that police were not entirely satisfied with Blake's version of events. The source also told the newspaper that police thought it strange that Harland Braun showed up so quickly. The source indicated that as far as the police were concerned, Blake was not off the hook.

In the meantime, the authorities announced that the results of Bonny's autopsy would remain sealed at the request of homicide detectives who were concerned that their release might serve to hinder their investigation. They followed a similar procedure in their handling of the murders of Nicole Simpson and Ronald Goldman in 1994, much to the frustration of the public and reporters.

"We're conducting the investigation in a proper manner, and we're trying to ensure that it's handled right and everyone's rights are protected," Tatreau announced.

On Sunday, May 6, Blake hired a private investigator to try to solve his wife's murder. According to

Braun, a private investigations firm began searching the bungalow where Bonny lived behind Blake's residence and going through her personal belongings and papers in search of clues that might shed some light on who killed her.

"Our investigators are now searching the house after the LAPD finished," Braun said. "With our assistance, there may be stuff in her property that could provide clues . . . the police didn't really have a chance to understand her background, so there may be a clue that we can find that they didn't." Braun said that Blake would turn over anything that was found to the police, and that he had remained cooperative with the investigators. "Obviously a murder case remains open until it is solved."

Braun revealed that Bonny had a criminal history and had been on probation in Arkansas. According to court records, Bonny had a conviction for a drug violation in 1989. In 1995 she had been charged in Tennessee for misrepresentation of the value of property, but she eventually pleaded guilty to a lesser charge. She had also been arrested in Arkansas in 1998 and was accused of being in possession of false identification and 16 stolen credit cards. She had pleaded guilty to misuse of a Social Security number and was placed on probation. Braun also reiterated that she had been involved in bilking lonely men out of money through ads placed in newspapers around the country in what he termed, "lonely hearts con schemes."

"She claimed that she had stopped it," Braun said. He indicated, however, that evidence was beginning to turn up in her residence and elsewhere that she had still been involved in the schemes right up to the time of her murder.

As one day turned into another, additional information about Bonny Bakley continued to surface as her friends and relatives began speaking out publicly about her lifestyle, her marriage and relationship with Blake, and her murder. Many said that she was obsessed with celebrities and had been involved in relationships with Dean Martin before his death in 1995, Frankie Valli, and others, including rock 'n' roll legend Jerry Lee Lewis. A number of people said that Bonny had claimed to have a daughter fathered by Lewis in the early 1990s, who she named Jeri Lee Lewis. Lewis, however, has denied being the child's father.

An attorney in Arkansas who represented Bonny after her arrest in 1996 claimed that the office of parole and probation had conducted an investigation that had confirmed that Bakley and Lewis had in fact had a child together. But Lewis insisted that it was not true, and claimed that he could prove by his passport and other documents that he was out of the country during the period in which the child would have been conceived. Similarly, Bonny's passport would show that she had not left the country to be with Lewis during the time in question. Furthermore, according to Lewis's former agent, Al Embry, Bonny dropped a paternity suit against Lewis prior to DNA testing.

Lewis's sister, Linda Gail Lewis, also a singer, who had at one time become a close friend of Bonny's after they met each other in 1986, recalled that Bonny had aggressively pursued her brother, also known as "The Killer."

"She'd do anything to be around my brother," Linda said. "I don't know how she met so many famous people. She got to know Frankie Valli, Dean Martin, and Christian Brando . . . Bonny may have had enemies. She was a darker, more sinister version of Kate Hudson's character [a star-seeker in the movie *Almost Famous*]. There was no stopping Bonny. She was relentless . . . Bonny had enough charm that you'd put up with things she did."

Yet another attorney, Cary Goldstein, soon entered the picture. Goldstein, who once represented Bonny in the paternity and prenuptial matters involving Blake, was now representing the interests of some of Bonny's family members. He painted a different picture of the slain woman.

"In my dealings with her," Goldstein told *The Los Angeles Times*, "she was nothing but honest, decent, and honorable. She was never deceptive, and had a lot of character. I have no doubt that she was a good woman. I liked her as a person . . . I'm very troubled by the fact that her husband, within hours of her murder, finds it necessary to put deeply personal background information about my client into the media. I question his motives. I'm deeply troubled by his criticisms of the Los Angeles Police Department investigation. My question is: Why are they doing this? Why is he trashing his wife in the national media?"

The details of the prenuptial agreement on which Goldstein assisted Bonny, signed by both parties on

October 4, 2000, a little more than a month before
their marriage, was an unusual one. Blake had insisted
on the agreement after having a private investigator
delve into her background. The agreement, in part,
included a promise by Bonny that she would not conduct any "business" on Blake's property or otherwise
involve Blake in her business activities. She was also
forbidden to associate with "known felons" while she
was with baby Rose, and she was to keep the baby
away from any illegal drug use or activities.

CHAPTER 4

BASED ON ADDITIONAL INFORMATION DEVELOPED BY Captain James Tatreau's team of homicide detectives, approximately 30 police officers, some in plain clothes, converged on Robert Blake's Dilling Street home shortly after nine P.M. Wednesday, May 9, 2001, where they executed a second search warrant. A prepared statement was released to the media.

"Robbery-Homicide personnel served an additional search warrant on the residence of Mr. Robert Blake as part of their ongoing investigation into Bonny Bakley's murder," an LAPD spokesperson told the media. "The search warrant was affected as the result of new information received by the concerned detectives on May 8, 2001. Specific items of evidence were sought. No one has been ruled out as a suspect or suspects in the murder of Ms. Bakley."

"We have certainly not ruled out Mr. Blake," Tatreau said. "We have not been able to develop enough evidence . . . as far as eliminating Mr. Blake, that takes us in another direction."

Although they would not elaborate, the police said that the decision to search Blake's home again was made following a police interview a day earlier, on Tuesday, May 8.

The search warrant covered both the primary residence and the bungalow in the rear, and included a demand that any and all items taken from the premises of either dwelling be turned over to the police. Apparently Blake's attorney and his private investigators had removed a number of items, including many of Bonny's personal possessions and papers. Blake's attorney, Harland Braun, assured the detectives that all of the items that had been removed would be delivered to police headquarters by the following day.

"We want the LAPD to investigate Robert Blake," Braun said, "because the more they investigate, they'll find out that he didn't do it."

Braun indicated that he and his client were taking comfort in knowing that the investigators were making an active attempt to recover any evidence that might lead to identifying Bonny's killer.

"Mr. Blake's actually very happy," Braun said. "He was a little concerned that the police weren't interested in anyone other than him, that they weren't looking at all this evidence." The evidence Braun referred to was apparently comprised of Bonny's personal papers and other items related to her past. "Now that they want it, he's really elated." Braun added that Blake remained very focused on catching his wife's killer.

"He knows in some ways that he will never be completely vindicated until a killer is apprehended and tried and convicted," Braun continued, "and so in that sense, he has his reputation at stake, knowing that if we don't find the killer, there'll always be a cloud over him. I think someday we'll know who the real killer is, because usually the guy gets drunk at a bar somewhere, brags, does something, and there's no statute of limitations on murder . . ."

Blake was not at home at the time and was believed to be staying with his daughter, Delinah, a psychologist, at her home in the exclusive area of Hidden Hills. News helicopters circled the actor's home from the air, while a mix of about 50 people made up of neighbors, additional police officers, and several reporters gathered in the street in front of his home trying to get any information they could.

It was revealed that among the items seized during the two searches performed at Blake's and Bonny's residences were two 9mm handguns, at least 100 rounds of ammunition, phone records, credit card-receipts, and various other papers. They were also looking for financial records of Blake's because detectives had been told about several substantial cash withdrawals that were essentially unaccounted for, and they also wanted Bonny's diary. Detectives apparently had received information indicating that Bonny's friends and family members contended that, in the diary, Bonny had detailed threats, purportedly made by Blake, against her. When the detectives were finished with their second search, it was well into the early morning hours of the next day. They carried out several large bags of evidence from Blake's property, including a large shopping bag and a white garbage bag, and took them to police headquarters. They also called in a tow truck and removed Bonny's car, a blue Mercedes that had been parked in Blake's backyard. However, they had not found Bonny's diary and hoped that it would be among the things Harland Braun world turn over.

In the meantime, Bonny's half brother, Peter Carlyon, a Tennessee resident, began speaking out about Bonny's relationship with Blake, a relationship that had purportedly caused her to express fear for her life to family members. Carlyon told reporters that Bonny had said that Blake had threatened her recently. According to Carlyon, Blake purportedly told Bonny during an argument that there was no need to worry about life getting her down because he "had a bullet with her name on it." Carlyon told a Memphis, Tennessee television reporter that Blake "was making a lot of verbal threats."

"I've heard all the things on the news about how he was carrying a gun because his wife feared for her life," Carlyon said. "She didn't want him carrying that gun." Carlyon said that Bonny had told relatives that, contrary to Blake's claims, she had asked Blake not to carry a gun.

Carlyon also said on national television that he was aware that his sister had sold nude photographs of herself over the Internet, went by at least 14 aliases, and had asked numerous lonely men for money. Saying that she was no angel, he contended that she did not deserve to be murdered.

Bonny's mother, Marjorie Lois Carlyon, publicly accused Blake of having been abusive, claiming that their baby daughter, Rose, was a continuing source of friction between them. Some friends and relatives said that Blake wanted to keep Rose away from Bonny despite a custody agreement, and they believed that he would have killed Bonny in order to keep the child.

"I just said that if I were you, I would let him have that baby and let him raise it and get away from him," Bonny's mother said.

John Solari, a close friend of Blake's, indicated that Blake was unhappy and even miserable in his marriage with Bonny. However, Solari stressed that Blake would not have harmed his wife or had her killed. On one occasion, Solari said in a shocking statement on ABC News and in *The Free Republic*, he had offered to kill Bonny himself, but that Blake had flatly turned down the offer.

"I said, 'Robert, I'll take her off the count, please,' " Solari said that he told Blake. "He says, 'John, I can't do that. I gotta make this work.' "

Although it would not be reported to the public for more than a week, earlier that same day, Monday, May 7, detectives Juan Parga, Dan Jenks, and Michelle Harvey spent a great deal of time working around the area where Blake had parked his Dodge Stealth the night Bonny was murdered. Although they would not tell reporters what they were doing or looking for, it was obvious that they were searching for clues. They carefully looked through and removed items from three large garbage receptacles at a construction site, close to where Blake had parked the night of the murder. Nearby, presumably before the police had taped off the area to identify it as a crime scene, a number of unknown people had placed a variety of flowers atop a utility box near the sidewalk as a memorial of sorts to Bonny.

At one point, Parga carefully removed a small item that, from a distance, appeared to be a gun. It was later revealed that they had indeed found a gun, and they eventually confirmed that it was found inside one of the trash bins that they had been searching. The gun, it turned out, was a rare German Walther PPK pistol. There was little doubt that they had found the murder weapon. It had been freshly oiled, and from initial appearances the investigators doubted that they would be able to lift fingerprints from it.

Garrett Zimmon, commanding officer of the LAPD's Detective Services, later said that the details being reported, including details about the gun, were little more than media rumors, nothing more, and reassured the public that detectives were doing a thorough job of investigating the case. They would neither confirm nor deny any of the reports that had been appearing in the media.

"They are looking at all possible evidence and interviewing any and all witnesses," Zimmon said. "Contrary to some rumors, there is no pending arrest of a suspect in this case." Zimmon cautioned the media about making harsh judgments about Bonny Lee Bakley because of what was being reported, stressing that doing so could make it more difficult for the investigators to do their jobs, especially when it came to interviewing witnesses. "We must remember that Bonny Lee Bakley is not the one under investigation. She is the victim. We need to be sensitive to that."

"We're not commenting on evidence collected or

not collected," said LAPD police spokesman Sergeant John Pasquariello. "This is a sensitive investigation and everyone should understand that . . . we are not going to investigate a murder case in the media."

Harland Braun, meanwhile, said that he had information about the gunpowder residue tests and other tests from sources that he would not identify. They showed that Blake was "clean." Countering the media reports that the tests had come back as "inconclusive," Braun said, "It's not inconclusive, it's negative."

"If they had gunshot residue tests that showed anything on him, he would be in custody by now," Braun said. Referring to the Walther PPK that had been found, he went on to say that he believed that a hit man, possibly hired by someone out of Bonny's past, had killed her.

"I thought that they had a gun," Braun said, "because they seemed to lose interest at some point in the other guns [out of Blake's collection] . . . it is fairly common for assassins to dump the gun. I'm working on the hit man theory . . . Bonny's death is consistent with a hit man. It's not my client, so it has to be a hit man." Blake, he said, was shocked when he learned that he was being investigated for his wife's murder.

"He's grieving, he's scared, they're investigating him for murder," Braun said. "He's got his wife's family accusing him of murder, he's got a daughter, an 11-month-old child, he's got her family members out there acting strangely."

When asked about the writing on the wall in Blake's home—I'M NOT GOING DOWN FOR THIS—

Braun initially said that he had not seen the writing himself and therefore knew nothing about it. However, at a later press conference, Braun said that those words had been there for more than a year and indicated that they were written as part of Blake's prior psychoanalysis therapy in which it had been suggested that he write down his feelings.

"That's something that's been on his wall for more than a year and it has nothing to do with this case," Braun said. "It's just a fighting slogan, like 'don't let the bastards get you down.' "

He didn't say why he thought Blake would have written the words on a wall inside of his house rather than a piece of paper, but it was suggested that if they were written on a wall they would serve as a better reminder to what Blake was trying to say because the slogan would be in plain view.

On Thursday, May 10, Braun, as promised, delivered three trunks, six suitcases and three file boxes of documents, photographs, and audiotapes to LAPD headquarters. Braun described Bonny as a "packrat" who kept a large number of papers and other documents relating to her scams. Braun said that the items he turned over to the police included, among other things, "the lonely hearts thing, articles about her going back to the early '70s, pictures of her in the '70s, phony pictures of her with Elvis Presley, and other stars." There were even tabloid magazines that dated back to the 1980s, filled with stories about the celebrities she had gone after. Little had she known that she, herself, would make headline news in the very same tabloids after her murder. In a sense she had achieved the fame that she had long been seeking—it was just too sad that she achieved it after death.

"There is all types of things I think the police could possibly use in a very difficult investigation," Braun said. "They need every scrap of evidence they can get."

The police did not find the diary they were looking for among Bonny's things, according to news reports. Braun did not indicate whether it was among the items that he turned over to the police.

There were a number of letters among her belongings, however, including form letters Bonny used in her lonely hearts scams: she described herself to men as being young, slim, and single and she asked them to send her money.

An 82-year-old widower claimed to have sent her $250 on April 2, 2001 for plane fare when she wrote to him and gave him a story about being down on her luck.

"She made me feel sorry for her," said the widower, who was from the Boston, Massachusetts area and who did not want to be identified. "I told her there were some jobs out here in Kingston. I sent her plane fare. She never came. I guess I got fooled."

The man said that she kept the money and never showed up. When he realized that he had been scammed, he claimed that he wrote her a letter on April 10, 2001 that began, "Dear Swindler: The thing that hurts the most is that Bonnie [sic] Bakley is a thief."

Later, Braun released to the media a number of audiotape recordings that Bonny had made of telephone conversations with others. In one she discussed with a friend whether or not she should leave Christian Brando for Robert Blake.

"I thought he was cute when he was younger . . . I thought, well, when I met Blake I kinda wanted him but I kinda didn't because he wasn't like up to par with the looks," Bonny is heard saying to a friend identified only as Ray. "I thought, well, I don't know if I really would want him the rest of my life because he's going to get even older and worse looking and I'm already in love with Christian . . . who would you go for? Blake or Christian? I'd probably feel more safe with Blake."

"Blake ain't gonna let you hustle him," Ray responded. "Blake's too slick."

"You think Blake is like a genius?" Bonnie asked.

"I think he's hip," Ray said. "You ain't gonna get a dime out of him . . . he's not a dummy. I think he's going to use you more than you use him."

"What would he use me for?" Bonny asked.

"Just sex," responded her friend. A baby can be heard in the background as they talk.

"I don't know if the baby is going to work for or against me," Bonny said. "Some guys don't like having a kid squalling around. They get on your nerves." She stated that she wasn't sure Christian Brando would like having a baby around for that reason.

"Is it really his [Brando's] baby?" Ray asked.

"Yeah."

"Are you certain?"

"Yeah."

"Bonny, did you ever try to figure out why you're attracted only to famous people?" Ray asked.

"It's because I wanted to be that myself," she responded. She went on to say that she was an outcast in school, in part because she came from a poor family and did not dress as well as the other kids. "You think, 'I'll show them. I'll become a movie star.' But it's too hard . . . if I'd kept romance out of my life it would have been possible. But I would have had to be like Katharine Hepburn and it was too hard. I kept falling for somebody. So I thought, why not fall for a movie star instead of being one. It's more fun. I like being around celebrities. It makes you feel better than other people."

After the tapes were made public, Cary Goldstein, who was hired by Bonny's family members, blasted Braun on NBC's *Today* by saying that his behavior was "disgraceful." He accused Braun of attempting to smear his deceased client, herself a murder victim, in what he viewed as an obvious attempt to "taint the [potential] jury pool. He referred to her as Lee Bonny because that was the name he had known her by.

"Before Lee Bonny's body was even cold," Goldstein said, "here's Mr. Blake's attorney trashing her on the national media, pulling skeletons out of the closet about her past."

Her second husband, Robert Moon, who was married to Bonny from 1985 to 1987, went on the national television tabloid show *Extra* and described some of Bonny's mail-order operations while they were married. Moon hinted that someone from her past might have killed her.

"I told her years ago . . ." Moon said. "Somewhere down the road, someone's going to kill her . . . because she's playing everybody."

There were skeletons indeed, as would soon be seen.

CHAPTER 5

BACKGROUND INFORMATION GATHERED BY THE LOS Angeles Police Department, as well as by Blake's own private investigators, showed that Bonny Lee Bakley was born on June 7, 1956 in historic Morristown, New Jersey, the eldest child in a working class family and daughter of a tree surgeon.

Morristown is situated just west of Newark along Interstate 287, between Parsippany and Basking Ridge near the Great Swamp National Wildlife Refuge. Nowadays, with a population of approximately 17,000, Morristown is considered a good place to raise kids and supports an interesting, and historic environment. The Morristown Historical Park preserves sites of historical value in an area that had once been occupied by General George Washington and the Continental Army. One of Morristown's most striking landmarks is the Jacob Ford Mansion, which Washington used as his military headquarters during the winter of 1779–1780. But Morristown is a quiet, sleepy little town with little to do for those who seek the excitement of a neon nightlife. As such, Bonny didn't much like it there, and she began dreaming early in her life of how she would escape the confines of small-town life. She wanted to break away from the terrible memories: she claimed to have been sexually abused by her father at age seven. (She would later say that he died before she became old enough to kill him.) Her fantasies of stardom helped squelch those memories, for a while.

Her dreams of breaking into show business actually began in high school where they remained just that— dreams. After high school, however, she made her first attempt to make those dreams a reality when she did a brief stint as a model. She went to New York with aspirations of becoming an actress and hitting it big. However, Bonny's dreams never came to fruition and she ended up marrying a man named Paul Gawron, a laborer, by the time she was in her mid-twenties. She had two children with Gawron, Holly and Glenn, both of whom are now in their twenties. But her relentless obsession with celebrities and her aspirations for stardom were insatiable and, shortly after starting a mail-order business in 1982 that would later become a major part of her lonely hearts scams, she and Gawron divorced.

Bonny soon befriended a would-be rocker in Palisades Park, New Jersey named Robert Stuhr. He apparently had some peripheral connections in the movie industry. Stuhr managed to get Bonny and his own daughter parts as extras in the 1985 movie, *Turk 182*, which starred Robert Urich and Timothy Hutton. The part in the movie led nowhere, but Bonny persevered. Her friend Stuhr also ran a music company called Norway USA, and she recorded some songs that were considered by many to be absolutely awful. One of the songs was called "Rock-A-Billy Love," and another, recorded under the name of Leebonny Bakley, was called "Tribute to Elvis Presley" and contained a line in the lyrics that read, "Rock and roll will never be the same, Rock and roll Leebonny is my name." Years earlier, in the 1970s, she recorded another song that was just as bad, if not worse. The only difference was that the 1970s song, "Just a Fan," turned out to be somewhat prophetic if judged by the song's lyrics: "I am chasing a celebrity . . . there's no future in it I can see." (There was a recent attempt to auction an authenticated copy of "Just a Fan" on eBay after her death, with a minimum bid of $1,000. However, after ten days the bidding was closed without a single bid having been received.)

By 1990 Bonny found herself in Memphis, Tennessee, where she was determined to meet her idol, Jerry Lee Lewis.

"She was a groupie and she really wanted to meet my brother," said Lewis's sister, Linda Gail Lewis. "And she did."

Linda Gail Lewis, who recently recorded an album with Van Morrison, said that she and Bakley somehow met, but she could not recall how or where. Lewis said that she and Bonny became close friends until Bonny began telling everyone that Jerry Lee Lewis had gotten her pregnant.

"I was playing music at night, and sometimes Bonny would come over and her kids would swim in the pool with mine," said Linda Gail. She said that she did not understand what her brother could have seen in Bonny because by the time Bonny met him she had become considerably overweight and had two children that she was trying to raise. "I don't know if the DNA tests proved the little girl was his baby. But I think there was some settlement."

Bonny's daughter, Jeri Lee Lewis, father undetermined, was born on July 28, 1993, in Desoto County, Mississippi.

"Bonny was always dating somebody, even celebrities like Dean Martin," said Linda Gail. "She called me up one night [in early or mid-1995] really excited and said she was out with Dean Martin. She put him on the phone, and the guy on the other end sounded like Dean . . . the last time I saw Bonny was three years ago in Memphis, when she came to one of my gigs. She was spending every weekend in a penal farm and seeing Christian Brando. She didn't tell me how she hooked up with him, but I was amazed by it."

Despite the other celebrities she had dated, Bonny seemed obsessed with Jerry Lee Lewis. Lewis's other sister, Frankie Jean Lewis, told investigators that Bonny's intentions toward "The Killer" were always out in the open.

"She had sworn to marry him," said Frankie Jean, who runs the Jerry Lee Lewis family museum in Ferriday, Louisiana. "She told everyone that she would. Jerry would just smile."

On May 8, 2001, Jerry Lee Lewis and his family issued the following statement, portions of which appeared in newspapers around the country, regarding Bonny Lee Bakley:

"Because of the statements and false allegations reported recently in the media concerning a 'relationship' between Jerry Lee Lewis and Bonny Lee Bakley Blake, we feel we need to make a statement correcting inaccurate information being fed to the public.

"First and foremost, we offer our deepest condolences to Mr. Robert Blake and his family, as well as Mrs. Blake's family. As saddened as we are to hear of anyone dying, we want it made clear that I have never fathered a child by Mrs. Robert Blake, Bonny Lee Bakley, to whom my name has been attached since her murder has been reported in the media over the last few days.

"Years ago, Mrs. Blake was an avid fan, but after some time, she began harassing my family while, at the same time, she was married and living in New Jersey. She moved to Memphis in the hope that I would leave my devoted wife, Kerrie, and our son, Jerry "Lee" Lewis III, and marry her: merely a figment of her own imagination. Mrs. Blake then went on to cultivate friendships with my relatives and friends, hoping somehow this would help her cause. However, her stalking of my family, as well as her threats to kill our son, landed her in a Memphis courtroom. As a last-ditch attempt to form a relationship with me, in 1993 she charged she was carrying my child and stories to this effect appeared in the tabloids. This claim was thrown out of a Memphis courtroom as our lawyer proved, with my passport, that I was out of the country longer than her records claimed she was pregnant. Since she had no records to show she had left the country, the case was over before it began. I know I am a strong man, but this I could not have done!

"That is the last I ever heard of her, other than that she continued to show up at a few of my concerts over the years.

"I do hope the child who has my name and has been told I am her father learns that I am not her father and that I am very sorry that she has had to suffer this lie. I have always taken care of my children and have never denied any of my children. I have lost two sons already. The lives of my children are very dear and precious to me!!

"I do hope these truths will put an end to questions concerning my involvement with the life and death of Bonny Bakley Blake.

"Sincerely, Jerry Lee Lewis and Family."

When Bonny decided that it was time to finally move on, she left her daughter, Jeri Lee, with her former husband, Paul Gawron. However, she sent money to Gawron on a regular basis to aid in supporting the girl. By then her mail-order scams were in full swing.

A closer scrutiny of Bonny's criminal history showed that she was first arrested in 1989 in Memphis on a misdemeanor drug charge and was fined $300. She got into trouble again seven years later, in 1995, on the charge of misrepresentation of the value of property. When the detectives dug deeper, they learned specifically what those charges entailed. Bonny had been caught attempting to pass two bad checks, one for $600,000 and another for $2,000, drawn on the account of a Memphis record company. After she plea-bargained the offense down to lesser charges, she was sentenced to three years doing weekend work on a penal farm and was fined $1,000. Three years later in 1998, shortly after completing her sentence in Tennessee, Bonny was caught in Arkansas with seven driver's licenses and five Social Security cards, all with different names. According to one of Blake's private detectives, Scott Ross, Bonny was using the fake identification to rent post office boxes at various locations around the country from which she could run her lonely hearts scams and bilk men of varying ages out of cash in amounts that ranged anywhere from $20 to $200, sometimes even more. It was through such scams, contended Blake's lawyer, that Bonny had made a lot of enemies over the years, some of whom may have had a motive to kill her.

The detectives turned up information that showed that Bonny also advertised for male companions in a number of magazines. Those who responded were sent letters, many of them form letters that Bonny had set up, asking for money. According to private investigator Scott Ross, the police found dozens of envelopes containing small bills inside her bungalow from men around the country and from other parts of the world, some from Germany and the Netherlands. There were also a number of the lonely hearts advertisements that she had placed in magazines that described her as a "young, single pretty girl." One of the ads read: "I can travel if you can't in order to meet. I'm sad and lonely due to a recent breakup with someone I was engaged to, need your letters to cheer me." On Saturday, May 5, the day after she was murdered and prior to the second police search, Federal Express delivered two boxes of mail addressed to Bonny.

The police also discovered nude photographs of a woman—they were not of Bonny—that Bonny had sent to a number of men claiming they were photographs of her. The police also found a number of handwritten lists detailing men's names, telephone numbers, addresses, and amounts of money that they had sent her. There were also memos written to herself beside the entries that included aliases that she had used in the letters to the men—reminders so that she wouldn't get them mixed up—and details of each man's likes and dislikes such as, "loves phone sex."

Less than two weeks before being murdered, Bonny sent one of her form letters to a 46-year-old man in Van Nuys, California in which she wrote that she was being evicted from her apartment and needed $150 to $200 for rent money. She added that she would accept $20, however, so that she could play the state lottery. She also wrote: "Don't worry, I'm not fat, I promise I never will be. I'm into sex with the right man who I want to have a relationship with. I do hope it's going to be you." She signed the letter, "Miss Lee Blakely." The Van Nuys man never bought her story and never sent her any money.

"This woman made a lifetime out of bilking lonely men," Ross said. "She had it down to a science."

Although it was obvious that the cops were still focusing on Robert Blake as their prime suspect in Bonny's murder, they agreed that the motive for her murder could lie in her past because of the number of enemies she had made over the years. With all the evidence to that effect in her home, it would have been foolish to deny the possibility.

As the investigation into Bonny's murder continued, a more sordid picture of the slain woman began to emerge. From many of her letters it appeared as if she had a voracious sexual appetite that bordered on addiction. She was kinky, and bragged that she had participated in orgies, sadomasochism, and lesbian acts in order to satisfy her desires. She wrote that she was uninhibited and enjoyed nearly every type of sexual pleasure that could be imagined. She advertised as much, and set up dates with men interested in sampling her repertoire. She claimed that she had been raped during one encounter, and that had prompted her to stop providing her address and phone number to men.

Leading up to that encounter, she said that she had received a letter and a photo from a man who appeared to be nice. After setting up a date with him, she claimed that he was grossly overweight, had rotten teeth, and lived in a filthy apartment. Although she had attempted to get away from him, she failed, and he forced her to do the perverted things that he wanted. When she was allowed to leave, she was badly bruised from having been beaten by the man.

That brush with danger didn't stop her, however. According to her many writings, she continued to contact men through ads and the mail, often boasting that she would try anything sexual at least once. She spoke of her many sexual toys, including a vibrating egg and other vibrators, and continued to talk about liking sadomasochism, bondage and dominance, ménage à trois, and sex with other women. She claimed that she was bisexual and liked to "swing" with couples where the woman was also bisexual. As was her custom she would ask the men for varying denominations of money, depending upon the sexual scenario. Often she would not show up for the dates that she had arranged and would keep the money that had been sent to her. According to friends, when she did show up it was only to satisfy her sexual cravings. Friends said that she'd had hundreds of lovers over the years.

Information surfaced that indicated that Bonny also liked the club scene, and would hang out at nightclubs until the early morning hours. She even admitted to friends that she was leading a dangerous lifestyle, and said that she would probably meet a man one day who would end up killing her.

CHAPTER 6

ROBERT BLAKE WAS BORN MICHAEL GUBITOSI ON September 18, 1933 in Nutley, New Jersey. He had an abusive alcoholic father and a mother who showed him little affection. He was soon dubbed "Mickey," a name that would stay with him until executives at a major motion picture studio advised him to change his name to Robert Blake. Blake's parents, James and Elizabeth Gubitosi, performed a song-and-dance routine to try and make ends meet, all the while holding onto dreams that they could put their children into show business and that their children's successes, particularly Mickey's, might replace their own failures. It was in that vein that they decided to move Mickey, still a toddler, and his two older siblings, a brother and a sister, to Los Angeles where they were determined to get them into the movies.

They succeeded, but it wasn't until 1939, while Mickey was still five-years old. He began appearing in MGM's *Our Gang* series of short features as "Little Mickey," and was billed under his own name of Mickey Gubitosi. He worked regularly for a few years until he had grown out of the child role that the *Our Gang* series had called for. However, he was more fortunate than most child actors in that he continued to work, albeit sporadically, despite the problems he faced at home. Sexual and physical abuse, not to mention the psychological abuse that went along with them, were regularly inflicted on his young, impressionable mind and body by his parents. Beatings were a regular occurrence, creating a life of desperation and disparity for young Blake.

"They locked me in a closet and left me there all day long," Blake told a reporter in the early 1990s. "They made me eat on the floor like a dog ... my parents were committably insane."

His father died at age 48, and when he grew older Blake became estranged from his mother and had no communication with her for 30 years. She died in the late 1980s without ever patching things up with her son.

"My father was a sadistic madman and alcoholic who killed himself when he was 48 years old," Blake said. "My mother was equally bad, if not worse, because she saw what was happening and did nothing about it. She even encouraged him to lock me in closets for days, to tie me up like a dog, to make me eat on the floor, to sexually abuse me. . . . My whole life was being a whipping boy for a very diseased, terrible household . . . I lived in a terrible asylum, and they wanted me dead. That's where I came from . . . Every time anything good happened to me," Blake said, "I had to throw it away and say, 'Don't worry. I'll be garbage. Even in your grave you don't have to worry. I'll remain garbage so you'll be happy.' "

In the 1940s Blake obtained work as the Indian boy, "Little Beaver," in the very popular Western series, *Red Ryder*. In 1948 he landed a small part as a little

Mexican beggar, merely a boy, in the movie, *The Treasure of the Sierra Madre*, with Humphrey Bogart in which he tries to sell Bogart's character a Mexican lottery ticket. It was a small part, but it helped keep his name alive in the industry that, in turn, kept him working.

Despite his success in films as a child, Blake grew up in a poor community. Raised as a Catholic and a practitioner of the faith until he was about 16, and having worked as an extra in *Going My Way* with Bing Crosby while still a child, Blake began hanging around with priests in downtown Los Angeles while still in his teens. He began thinking that he would like to play the part of a priest someday. Little did he know at the time that he would.

Unable to cope with his anguish, anger, and pain, Blake enlisted in the army as an attempt to try and leave his past life behind. His deep-seated anger was still there, however, and it gave rise to more problems for the young man trying so desperately to find himself.

While stationed in Alaska, a lieutenant ordered him to clean up his messy footlocker. Blake refused.

"Watch this!" Blake recalled telling the lieutenant as he picked up the heavy footlocker and heaved it out of an upstairs barracks window. "Then I started laughing like a madman . . . I picked up the gun and was suicidal, so they put me in the nuthouse."

During his tour of military duty in Alaska, Blake fell deeply in love with a 16-year-old girl who lived near the base. Because the girl's father disapproved of the relationship and the fact that her father wanted

Blake prosecuted for statutory rape for having sex with the girl, Blake, again by his own admission, began plotting her father's murder.

"I know firsthand how it feels to have the mind of a killer, because I nearly became a murderer myself," Blake said. ". . . I went crazy. I just didn't know I was crazy. In a sense her father wanted to take my life. So in my mind, I decided to take his first."

After he had made the decision to commit the murder, Blake began stalking the girl's father, watching him at every opportunity.

"The night I went to do it," he continued, "I felt perfectly sane. I arrived at the trailer just before dark and sat inside, freezing to death, just waiting. I kept thinking, 'No one will know I did this.' Finally he came out, walked down the path and around the car. My heart raced with excitement. He put his keys in to open the door and had his back to me, no more than thirty feet away. I raised the gun and put my finger on the trigger. My hand was as steady as could be. I was going to kill him."

With his intended victim clearly in his gun's sights, Blake said that he saw the door of the house open, and out stepped the girl that he loved.

"She walked down the path and handed her father a Thermos he'd forgotten," Blake said. "And then she put her arms up to his shoulders and kissed him. The moment she kissed him, I said to myself, 'She loves him.' And something made me put the gun down. [She] went inside, her father drove off, and I went back to my barracks. It was over. But I have no doubt that if she'd opened the door three seconds later, I would have killed him."

Blake was 21 when he got out of the army and that, he said, is when "the shit really hit the fan." His childhood, what little he had of it, was by then legally over, and the few good memories he had of his early days had faded away. In his own words he claimed that he "was as close to being in a living hell as I ever want to get." He began to withdraw into himself, and would spend days at a time locked inside a room by himself, afraid to have contact with anyone and fearful of doing anything. Blake began to hate himself, and began having thoughts of suicide.

"I couldn't even get myself to go into a drugstore and buy a pack of razor blades to cut my wrists with . . ." Blake told *Playboy* magazine in an interview several years ago. ". . . I hated myself, hated everything. I felt useless and worthless, had no friends, no love, no career, no education, no parents, and no tomorrows. It all added up to nothing."

In his efforts to stop hurting himself and to try and develop self-love, something he had rarely if ever experienced, Blake entered psychotherapy. Although it was somewhat intensive, results did not come quickly. Blake was so drawn inward that his accomplishments came about in small steps, such as first being able to walk into a grocery store to buy something without fearing the person behind the counter. Before treatment there were times when he would wait until three or four o'clock in the morning to go to the store.

"I'd pick up something in a panic," he said, "put my money down, and then run out."

Although progress came slowly for Blake, it did come. By the time he was in his third year of therapy, Blake had overcome much of his fear and had established enough confidence to go into restaurants to eat on occasion.

"When I was finally able to go into a restaurant and feel like I had a right to pick up a menu and order a meal," Blake said, "Christ, it was like becoming a brain surgeon. I started doin' that and a whole lot of other things in the middle of my second year of therapy, and comin' into the third year, I was strokin'. I was studyin' acting full-time, doin' plays, workin', goin' to college at night and fuckin' everything that walked. I was cookin'!"

After he made significant progress in getting his life back together, Blake returned to television where he found work in supporting roles on *Fireside Theater* and other similar shows, all while he was still in his twenties. He also turned out a very fine performance in the 1959 film, *Pork Chop Hill*, and another in 1961's *Town Without Pity*.

That was also the year that he married actress Sondra Kerr. They had two children together, Noah and Delinah. Noah, now 36, is a singer and an actor, and Delinah, now 34, is studying for her doctorate degree in psychology. Sondra gave up acting for approximately six years after the children were born, but eventually returned to work. People at the time didn't think the marriage would last six months.

"Our marriage started out as a fuckin' 14-carat disaster," Blake once said. Despite a good deal of fighting and arguing, it looked like they might make it, for a while.

"... We'd get into terrible, sick fights and days of torturing each other with a lot of unhealthy dependency," Blake said. "Because we weren't able to live our own lives, we were being consumed by our neurotic needs rather than by our love. I expected all the things I didn't get as a kid from her, all of the things she needed, she expected from me. And, indeed, I tried to give them to her."

Nonetheless, the marriage didn't work, although it lasted longer than most Hollywood marriages. They separated in 1982 and were divorced the following year.

"The nature of their relationship was up, down, up, down," their son, Noah, said recently. "They were both very opinionated. It wasn't like Ozzie and Harriet."

As the decade of the 1960s continued and Blake and his wife tried to make the best of things, Blake, now into his thirties, found himself working on a number of Western television series that were popular at that time. After having been a guest star on the final season of *Have Gun, Will Travel* with Richard Boone, Blake became a regular on Boone's new series, *The Richard Boone Show*. Unfortunately, the new series only lasted one season and Blake found himself returning to television Western guest shots and occasional small parts in movies.

It wasn't until 1967, at 34-years-old, that Robert Blake finally earned the true respect that he deserved as an actor when he portrayed real-life killer Perry

Smith in the film adaptation of Truman Capote's *In Cold Blood*. That story depicted the utterly senseless and vicious murders of the Clutter family in Kansas in 1959. Blake's interpretation of the psychotic yet somewhat sympathetic Smith was so chilling and compelling that he won rave reviews and critical acclaim. But it didn't come without a price. He went into a deep depression afterward.

"What I felt Truman was really writing about in *In Cold Blood* was this," Blake told a *Playboy* interviewer. "Everybody knows what a murderer is a millionth of a second after he pulls the trigger. But what is he a millionth of a second *before* he pulls the trigger? I don't think anybody has an answer to it. It's not as simple as asking what makes a person kill or what the neurotic elements are that lead a person to become a murderer."

Despite the deep-seated personal problems Blake was going through after *In Cold Blood,* he went on to turn out a particularly good performance as an Indian fugitive in *Tell Them Willie Boy is Here* in 1969, and did an equally fine job in his portrayal of a motorcycle cop with a somewhat odious personality in 1973's *Electra Glide in Blue*, getting him a Golden Globe nomination for best actor in the dramatic-motion-picture category. However, in spite of his successes, Blake continued to battle his demons. Those demons eventually drove him to heavy drinking, popping pills, and a heroin addiction.

"I was strung out on heroin for two years, stole, smashed motorcycles into trees, boozed, ate pills by the handful," Blake said. "Self-destruction? I could write a book."

Nonetheless, Blake went on to get his own television series. When the actor of ABC's marginally successful *Toma* decided to call it quits, producer Joe Swerling Jr. brought in Robert Blake to fill his shoes in 1974. The show underwent a metamorphosis of sorts at that time. The locale was changed to California, a pet cockatoo named Fred was added, and the lead character and the show itself were both renamed *Baretta*. The newly revamped show debuted in January 1975 and became an almost instant hit. Blake even won an Emmy award that year for his performance as the lead character.

"Robert was always interesting to work with," said a screenwriter who worked with Blake, who added that Blake always wanted to change the scripts after they had been delivered. "I worked with him on *Baretta* and *Hell Town*, and knew him in between adventures in show biz. Robert's a very complex person. He had an obsession with the Moby-Dick story, and he wanted to do a story that had an echo of the Captain Ahab character . . . Robert always had a dark place within him where he wanted to go, and we had long discussions about this."

Blake's obsession with *Moby-Dick*, it seemed, stemmed from the childhood he lost to the movie industry and to the abuse he endured. In the Herman Melville classic, Captain Ahab lost his leg and a couple of boats to the great whale, and spent much of his life hunting him down. Blake's obsession paralleled Ahab's in that he spent a great deal of his life hunting down and trying to understand and defeat the demons that had wreaked so much havoc in his life. Every time he came close to achieving his goal, the demons always seemed to retreat into the ether. Like Ahab, Robert Blake has never been completely successful in putting down his demons.

However, Blake's demons would not let go of him in spite of his success. Already a perfectionist, he became more demanding and took on the network executives, producers, and screenwriters for more control over the show's production. He brought his wife, Sondra, aboard for a couple of episodes, and was belligerent and confrontational with the directors that he did not like.

"The Guild says you gotta have a director, so you stick a director in the chair," Blake said. "It's like sticking a broomstick in the chair. The show directs itself, anyway." He often ended up directing the show himself, even though an official director was on board. "Here at Universal, nobody listens and nobody cares," he once said. "As far as most people are concerned, they just as soon turn out Perry Mason or Donald Duck, it don't make no difference. 'Cause once you sell the hour, as long as it's on the air, it don't matter. You're on the air or you ain't on the air."

Blake's perfectionist attitude was often justified—he simply wanted to turn out a high-quality show, and many of the scripts and personnel brought to him weren't up to his standards. His attitude led to continuing battles with producers, screenwriters, and network executives—both on the set and off. He purportedly threatened to throw people out of windows, and on one occasion he allegedly chased a producer across a studio parking lot because the producer had substituted a script. He won a Golden Globe award for best television actor in a dramatic series for *Baretta* in 1976, and would later wonder how much of a role his substance-abuse problems played in his judgment calls.

Although *Baretta* had been in the top-ten in ratings at one point, the ratings began to slide and it never recovered despite day and time changes. Viewers loved his "Baretta says" type lines: "I told you, man, nobody kills nobody," said his Baretta character in an episode in which he had busted a killer. "That's the rules. I don't know no other way."

"He was a very tightly wrapped guy," said Stephen J. Cannell, creator of *Baretta*. "Very volatile . . . he hated the show, he hated the material we were sending him, he was rewriting constantly. He was very emotional, but I never saw him move it to the next level."

Despite the show's popularity, *Baretta* was canceled in 1978 after its eightieth episode. Many in the business blamed Blake for the show's downfall because of his frequent battling on the set, coupled with his substance-abuse problems, and he soon was labeled a troublemaker in the industry, making it difficult for him to obtain work in television.

On the set of a different show, another actor held up production because he kept forgetting his lines. The network sent a team of executives to the set to see what was holding everything up and, according to

Blake, the director blamed him instead of the actor who kept forgetting his lines.

"... This prick of a director points a finger at me!" Blake exclaimed. "I actually saw him do it. The network guys are yelling at him and he's pointing at me, so I go right up to 'em and say, 'I'm ready to go. I ain't havin' no fuckin' problems. I know my jokes and I'm ready, so let's shoot.' "

The director was incensed that Blake would dare go up against him in front of the network executives, and he confronted Blake about it. Blake told him he knew what he had told the executives, and a heated argument ensued. Blake, realizing that he needed to walk away from the situation, turned and headed for the door. But the director followed him, and when he put his hand on Blake's shoulder Blake turned around and knocked him to the floor, toppling a five-gallon water bottle off a water cooler. It landed on the director's chest.

Blake was persistent, however, and he continued to find work. In 1981 he starred in five made-for-television movies—in three of these he played Detective Joe Dancer—and produced and starred in a television remake of John Steinbeck's *Of Mice and Men*. The following year he hosted one installment of *Saturday Night Live*, and in 1983, the year he and Sondra divorced, he turned out an impressive performance as Jimmy Hoffa in the television movie, *Blood Feud*.

However, because of his reputation for causing problems on the set and for substance abuse, a stipulation was placed in his contract before he was given the Hoffa role—his money, as well as that of his producer, would be placed in an escrow account and could only be collected if he remained drug free, caused no problems on the set, and completed the project on time. Although Blake had steadfastly maintained that he was not using drugs, the production company's insurer refused to provide coverage for him without the stipulation. Blake came through with flying colors and received accolades from reviewers for his performance as well as a Golden Globe nomination.

In 1985, Blake's teenage desire to someday play the part of a priest came true when he signed on with NBC to portray Father Noah "Hardstop" Rivers in *Hell Town*. Blake portrayed a tough priest ministering to the gritty streets of East LA and was the show's executive producer. By that period of his life he was no longer abusing heroin, but he was eating unhealthy foods, popping sleeping pills regularly, and harbored a fear that he would kill himself. Mentally, he just couldn't seem to cut it.

"I would get in the limo to go to the *Hell Town* location every morning," he said, "and I'd be so uptight I could hardly breathe."

Blake decided he wanted out, and after 16 episodes *Hell Town* was canceled in December 1985. He also severed a long-standing relationship with a talent agency and all but disappeared from the industry for the next eight years. It wasn't that he could not find work during that period—he just didn't want it.

During the periods when Blake nose-dived into depression and alcohol and drug abuse, he often drove up into the mountains where he would hole up for days on end in cheap motels, sometimes hanging out in the locals' pool halls.

"He fell apart and stayed there," said his daughter, Delinah.

Blake came out of his self-imposed hiatus from show business in 1993 and staged a comeback when he landed the title role in the television movie, *Judgment Day: The John List Story*, about a man who had killed his family, taken on a new identity, and evaded capture for twenty years. Again he had proven that he hadn't lost it yet, and won critical acclaim as well as an Emmy nomination for his performance.

Blake said that his portrayal of List was not a difficult role for him to assume.

"You have to love the person you are going to play," Blake said. "You can't say, well, this guy killed his family, I am going to play this ghoul. I have played a lot of people who killed. I have been on death row. You know, I have never met a murderer in my life. That's because there aren't any. There are people who crossed the line. Some of us don't cross the line."

After finding a new therapist, who helped him recall and learn to cope with his memories of the childhood abuse he had suffered, Blake seemed to make remarkable headway toward recovery. He often talked openly with the media about the dark side of his psyche that he had struggled with for so long.

"I could have gone either way," Blake told *People* magazine. "I could have wound up in a head-on collision, killing a family. I could have flipped out in some bar or restaurant some night and killed some-body."

In 1993 Blake underwent a much publicized face-lift operation in the mistaken belief that it would help him win more roles. Because he was not happy with the way the operation turned out, it was a decision he regretted.

"I survived my whole life by listening to my own drummer," the actor said regarding his decision to get a face-lift. "Then all of a sudden I said, 'Gee whiz, all the stars my age look like they belong on *The Donna Reed Show*, so I'll do it, too.' I'm sorry I gave in to that shit."

Two years later, in 1995, he turned out an easily forgettable performance as a transit authority chief in the feature film, *Money Train*, with Wesley Snipes and Woody Harrelson, and in 1997 he landed a role as "Mystery Man" in David Lynch's feature film, *Lost Highway*.

He has not worked since.

CHAPTER 7

As the investigation into Bonny Lee Bakley's mysterious death continued, considerable attention revolved around the discovery of the Walther PPK in the garbage bin by LAPD detectives Juan Parga, Dan Jenks, and Michelle Harvey. Considered a medium-caliber firearm, the PPK is a small, traditional double-action gun capable of firing both .380-caliber bullets and .32-caliber bullets. With an overall length of 6.25 inches, a height of four inches, and a width of a little more than an inch, and weighing only 21 ounces, the Walther it is relatively easy to conceal.

According to reports that appeared on ABC's *Good Morning America*, the gun had had three bullets in it, but two had been fired. One bullet was still in the chamber. It was also reported that the police had seized a box of ammunition, Remington Peters, a very common brand and the same brand found in the gun, during their initial search of Blake's home. Three bullets were missing from the box of ammunition taken from Blake's home. There was only one problem— and it was a big one—the casings on the bullets seized from Blake's home did not match the casing of the bullet found inside the Walther PPK. However, in the interim between when the gun was discovered and the time that this was reported a week later, the police had been able to determine that the bullet that killed

Bonny had been fired from the Walther PPK.

The Walther's serial number had been filed off, and the detectives knew that professional hit men often file off the serial numbers of the guns they use to make the weapon untraceable. Since rumors and speculation hinted that a hit man hired by someone out of her past might have killed Bonny, this was one avenue that was being explored. But in this case the number had been poorly filed, and when examined by the FBI, they were able to make it out. That, in the minds of the investigators, poured considerable cold water on the hit-man theory. It just didn't seem like a professional hit.

The autopsy report has not yet been released. We do not know whether Bakley was shot in the right side of the head or the left. That may prove critical to the case.

The driver-side window was rolled up when the police had arrived on the scene, and the detectives had been unable to find any witnesses to the actual shooting or, for that matter, anyone who might have heard her scream out of fear or cry out for help. Also, there was no evidence that Bonny had made any attempt at escape. As a result the detectives theorized that Bonny's killer would likely have been inside the car with her, sitting in the driver's seat, a strong indication that she knew and trusted the person who had killed her. They postulated that she would not have remained inside the car if a stranger had opened the door and got inside with her, or at the very least she would have made an attempt to escape.

But who could have done it? The cops wondered.

If Blake had done it in the manner that they theorized,
wouldn't he surely have been spattered with blood
blow-back from the bullet's entrance wound if he had
been that close to her? No one reported seeing a
bloody Robert Blake—not Sean Stanek, not Joseph
Restivo at Vitello's, not any of the customers or employees of the restaurant. If he had opened the driver's
side car door and stood back about four or five feet
and fired the weapon, it was plausible but not all that
likely that he would have avoided the blood blow-
back spatters when the bullet struck tissue and bone.
There would have likely been minute traces on his
clothing and/or face and hands that might not be visible to the naked eye, but these would have been revealed in the tests conducted later. It was possible that
the rolled up window and car door, if only opened
enough to allow room for a person's hand holding a
weapon, could have shielded the shooter from much
of the blood spatter. It could also help explain why
Bonny had been shot in the shoulder in that the
shooter might have had difficulty aiming the gun
within the limited and confined area of a partially
opened car door. This was, of course, mostly theory
and conjecture at this point, being fueled in part by a
frenzied media that was not receiving any information
from the police. Although the information surrounding Bonny's murder was officially being withheld
from the public, it eventually leaked out that Jenks,
Parga, and Harvey, as well as a number of other
LAPD detectives, determined that Bonny had been
shot from inside the car. Nonetheless, the reality of it
all was simply that there were a number of possibil-

ities with regard to how Bonny was shot as well as to who had shot her.

Meanwhile, with the weapon's serial number now identified, the LAPD detectives, who had assistance from the FBI and the Bureau of Alcohol, Tobacco and Firearms, traced ownership of the Walther PPK as far as they could. They hit a dead end when they learned that it had been sold at a gun show—no records of the transaction had been kept. Without a complete paper trail to follow, the detectives resigned themselves to the fact that it could have made it into anyone's hands by the time of Bonny's murder. One thing seemed certain: They had been unable to link the gun to Robert Blake. Or had they?

The National Enquirer quoted an unnamed police source, who supposedly provided its reporters with information about the case, who claimed that a man had sold Robert Blake a Walther PPK, complete with a full clip of ammunition, and he had contacted the detectives. Excited that the man might be the big break in the case that they had been looking for, the detectives were eager to interview him. Their hopes were quickly dashed, however, when the man was unable to provide the cops with any paperwork bearing the gun's serial number. Without it, there was no way that they could conclusively say that the Walther PPK that had been sold to Blake was the same weapon that they had in their possession.

Meanwhile, when it became public knowledge that LAPD was looking at Blake as their prime suspect in his wife's murder, a rather unusual thing occurred. O. J. Simpson offered, unsolicited, his advice on what

Blake should and should not do on the television show *Extra*. It would have been almost laughable if Blake's situation was not revolving around such a tragedy.

"I've got to admit, I was pretty fascinated when I heard about it," Simpson said. "My first reaction was an immediate feeling of compassion for him because I knew what he was about to go through. I was saying, 'Man, this poor guy. I hope they find who did it right away because the next week or two is going to be horrible for him, being under that veil of suspicion."

Simpson, who was acquitted of murdering his wife, Nicole Brown Simpson, and her friend, Ron Goldman, in a criminal trial, was held liable for their deaths in a civil trial before a jury. Simpson provided Blake with advice on how to handle all of the media attention and scrutiny that he was about to receive.

"Don't watch TV, Robert," Simpson said. "I know that watching TV is only going to frustrate him. That's all it's going to do." He also recommended that Blake's legal counsel should stop releasing unflattering details of his murdered wife's background. "My lawyers never revealed any information about Nicole that her friends hadn't already revealed. My lawyers were never the leader in any of that because they were told specifically, and we had a philosophy—'Nothing negative about Nicole.' " Simpson also advised Blake not to take a lie-detector test. "Do exactly what the Ramseys did. A lie-detector test can only hurt him. It can't help him."

"Yeah," quipped Simpson as he quoted some of the words from the *Baretta* theme song, "keep your eye on the sparrow. Don't do the crime if you can't do the time."

In true Hollywood fashion, while detectives worked feverishly around the clock trying to solve the case, Robert Blake's home as well as the crime scene were added to the itinerary of Crime Scene Tours. According to Lonnie Levine, a former LAPD crime analyst who runs the tours, the sites were added so quickly due to popular demand.

"We go by Vitello's restaurant," Levine said. "We retrace the steps that Mr. Blake went from the restaurant to the crime scene. We then drive by Mr. Blake's house just to show you the proximity of where the location was to his home . . . We're not in the business to show who's guilty or who's not. All we do is present the facts. And just the fact that he's very close to the restaurant, that was a favorite restaurant of his, that's why we think it's important."

The company's itinerary also includes the locations where Charles Manson's followers carried out their bloody crime spree, the location where Bill Cosby's son was slain, and a host of other locations where murders have occurred over the years. And, of course, the scene where Nicole Brown Simpson and Ronald Goldman were killed is included in the tour.

CHAPTER 8

As the investigation into Bonny Bakley's murder continued, the LAPD remained tight-lipped about any progress that they might be making. It was obvious that they were continuing to focus their attention on Robert Blake. Meanwhile Blake's lawyer, Harland Braun, tried to keep everyone's attention focused on Bonny's illegal activities in the hope that it would shake out new evidence that would move the police further from his client.

"They're overemphasizing Blake as a possible suspect," Braun said "Blake's position and my position is that he's innocent."

Although the LAPD would only say that Blake "has not been ruled out as a suspect," a New York newspaper reported that sources had indicated he was their prime suspect. The LAPD continued to remain equally evasive regarding any scientific evidence gathered in the case, particularly the gunshot-residue tests that had been performed on Blake and his clothing at LAPD's North Hollywood Division the night of the murder. The gun that the police believed had been used to kill Bonny had been sent to the Bureau of Alcohol, Tobacco, and Firearms' National Tracing Center in Falling Waters, West Virginia, where it would be thoroughly tested and traced and the results of it all would be sent to the LAPD when completed.

The LAPD also refused to release their own ballistics report to the public, and would likely do the same when the ATF's report came back.

"The last time I was briefed, they [the tests] had not come back," LAPD Chief Bernard Parks told CBS 2. Parks would only add that he had placed the department's best investigators on the case, and they were on it for a reason. He would not elaborate.

Amid media speculation that they were focusing primarily on Blake, the investigators, though remaining tight-lipped about the case, indicated that they were peering into Bonny's past as a con artist to see if one of her many victims may have had a motive to kill her. They also had a lot of questions they still wanted to ask Blake about his unusual and stormy relationship with his wife.

By May 11, Bonny's body was still in the custody of the coroner's office. Bakley's family's attorney, Cary Goldstein, was attempting to negotiate a $12,500 payment from Robert Blake to have Bonny's body shipped to her relatives and to pay for her funeral. Braun, however, indicated that before they agreed on an amount and shipped the body off, he and Blake would want to see the autopsy report. After reviewing the autopsy report, Braun said they might decide that they would want to have their own, independent autopsy performed. Goldstein clearly was not happy with the answers he was getting from Blake's camp.

"What is their daughter going to say when she's older and finds out that daddy was refusing to pay for mommy's funeral?" Goldstein asked. "We are appalled. Leebonny's body remains unclaimed and the

family finds it extremely distressing that Mr. Blake
has not agreed to pay reasonable funeral expenses."

"Leebonny loved the man," Goldstein added, "and
didn't understand why he was keeping her at a distance . . . she did care for him."

"Of course Robert's going to pay for his wife's
funeral," Harland Braun responded. "He's just not going to allow them to dictate to him what's going to
be done."

Even though the police weren't saying much about
the case, Bonny's family had plenty to say. They
came out and publicly stated that they did not think
Bonny's past as a con woman had anything to do with
her murder, and pointed the finger at Blake.

"He would be real nasty, and sometimes he would
be sweet," Bonny's mother, Marjorie Lois Carlyon,
said. "She liked him when he was sweet. I told her
that he's an actor, and how is she going to know when
he's acting."

According to Bonny's mother, Blake had inflicted
a great deal of physical and verbal abuse on Bonny,
much of it over their disputes about custody of their
baby daughter, Rose. Although they had a joint-
custody agreement, which was contingent upon
Bonny and Blake being married to each other by November 20, 2000, Blake purportedly wanted sole custody of the girl and didn't want Bonny around her.

The custody agreement had, among others, the following agreement within its body: "Mother shall not
conduct any business on Father's property and shall
not inform Father of any business and/or business activities that she conducts at any time and shall make

certain that no business arrangements of Mother shall involve Father at any time."

The custody agreement called for the provisions to end on February 1, 2001, at which time Bonny was due to be released from her probation in Arkansas for being convicted of possessing fake identification. It was reported that she was also under house arrest in Arkansas until that time and had been required to wear an ankle-monitoring bracelet. After February 1, 2001, the custody agreement called for Bonny and Blake to have equal access to Rose, and Blake's property, without further restrictions.

Blake also had a prenuptial agreement drawn up, her mother said, that in essence made her promise that she could not have friends or relatives visit her when she was on Blake's property. The couple, however, never signed it.

According to Bonny's family members, Bonny had used their child to threaten Blake on at least one occasion in which she had told him, "You'll never see our child again!" Bonny's family believed that it was his fear of losing little Rose that pushed Blake over the edge. Her family also said that Bonny had been fearful that Blake, or someone hired by him, would kill her. She was so fearful of her impending death, according to Bonny's sister, Margerry, that she began to secretly record their telephone conversations and hoped that if anything did happen to her it would be enough in incriminate Blake.

"He physically abused her, beat her up, and now he had her killed," her mother said. "Bonny said that

Blake was always threatening her. He told her, 'One day you're just going to disappear and nobody will ever find you!' He desperately wanted sole custody of their daughter and he was willing to do anything to get the girl, even if it meant killing Bonny Lee."

Judy Howell, a friend of Bonny's, told reporters as well as the police that, "Amazingly, the week before she was shot, Bonny told me Blake was even more bizarre than normal. Almost every day that week, Blake took Bonny around to different neighborhoods, 'looking for just the right spot,' he would mumble. Blake drove up and down different streets and if he found a spot he liked he pulled over, got out and told her to stay in the car while he looked around, like he was casing the area. Bonny asked him what he was doing, but he said, 'Just lookin' around. No big deal.' Bonny didn't know what to make of it."

Howell speculated that perhaps Blake had been searching for a place where he or someone else could murder Bonny without being noticed. ". . . I feel Blake is responsible," Howell said.

"I am 100 percent sure that Robert Blake was responsible for murdering my daughter," Marjorie Lois Carlyon told reporters, who were having a feeding frenzy with all of the information being provided by Bonny's friends. While it made for great reading material, readers could not help wonder how much of it was true and accurate.

Bonny, according to published reports, had done her homework nearly two years earlier, learning that Blake liked to hang out at a Los Angeles jazz club and the nights that he might be there. She traveled to Los Angeles with an entertainer friend and showed up at the club one evening in the autumn of 1999. Blake was there, and she made certain that she met him. For whatever reason, whether he was just lonely, drinking, or just couldn't pass up a potential opportunity with a woman, Blake took the bait and they ended up having sex. She had assured him that she was taking birth-control pills, but it would later be shown that she had in fact been taking fertility pills. She became pregnant, and nine months later Rose was born.

Bonny, though overweight and showing her age at the time of her death, had been beautiful in her youth. She wanted to avoid the trappings of a routine life like those of most people, particularly her sibling. Her sister, Margerry, works as a secretary in New Jersey. Her brother, Joey, works in construction in San Diego but lives in Tijuana, Mexico. Her half brother, Peter Carlyon, is in the landscaping business in Tennessee. She figured, correctly, that she could use her beauty to her advantage. Unfortunately, it may have also resulted in her death.

"She liked to live on the edge, that's for sure," Bonny's mother said. "I always worried about her."

The long and the short of it was simply that Bonny wanted to become a famous actress and hook up with a movie star.

"She was able to do half of that," Margerry, her sister, said. "Life can be hard."

Bonny was also an admirer of Donald Trump's, and she often dreamed of building an empire like his.

But they were just dreams—her efforts to attain wealth took her down a very different road than the one Trump had traveled.

"She adored [Trump]," her sister said. "Not for his looks but for his intelligence. She went out pursuing careers." While Bonny was out trying to find her niche in life and to make a name for herself, her husband, Paul Gawron, took care of their children. At one point, according to what she told her family, she obtained a Screen Actors Guild card and made a brief appearance in the movie *9½ Weeks*.

Bonny also worried a great deal about her looks and about being overweight. As with many women her age, she considered plastic surgery but never got around to having it done.

Her brothers and sister sometimes made fun of her endeavors toward stardom, like the time she placed an ad on a billboard in Hollywood in a failed attempt to obtain movie parts. But they were always grateful for the generosity she showed them.

"She would help the family out no matter what," her sister said. "If she didn't have the cash at the time, she would employ us."

Her family acknowledged that they were aware that she made her living investing in real estate, operating lonely hearts clubs that she referred to as dating services, and by selling nude photographs of herself by mail and on the Internet. She also always stayed in touch with them when she was away, and called Margerry nearly every night in the weeks prior to her death.

"Then she didn't call on Friday," Margerry said. She knew something was wrong because it wasn't like Bonny not to call, and then they found out a short time later that she had been killed.

According to Bonny's uncle, George Hall, Bonny had visited her friends and relatives in New Jersey about a month before her death. Following the trip, Hall said that one of Bonny's friends told him that her behavior was unusual at times during her visit, that she acted distraught and cried a lot.

"She mentioned [to her friend] that Blake wanted the baby but didn't want her," Hall said.

Bonny, according to relatives, refused to give up custody of Rose, and she and Blake were married on November 18, 2000. The wedding ceremony took place at Blake's home on Dilling Street, and was more an obligatory affair than a real wedding. Bonny was dressed in a white, mid-calf length dress, and Blake dressed in casual clothes. There was no food, no booze, not even champagne. Blake's grown children from his previous marriage, Noah and Delinah, did not attend. Blake's civil lawyer showed up, as did about a half-dozen friends. A few days after the wedding, Bonny returned to Arkansas to complete her probation there. Just before she left, Blake reportedly gave Bonny $100,000 as a buy-out incentive to stay out of Rose's life, and sent the child to live with his daughter in Hidden Hills.

When Bonny returned after completing her probation, according to her sister, Marjerry, she was not allowed to stay in Blake's primary residence but was required to stay in the guest house in back.

"She was totally embarrassed by that," Marjorie Lois Carlyon added. "And when he did allow her into the house, it was only for sex. Other times he would suddenly lose his temper and get really rough with her, often leaving bruises on her body. Bonny told me how Blake would grab and pull on her hair so hard she thought he was trying to pull it out in clumps. But Bonny stayed with him through it all. We all tried to talk to Bonny and convince her that Blake was a madman and capable of doing anything, but she refused to leave because she said he was a genius and that she loved him . . ."

Bonny purportedly had told her relatives that Blake, on the outside, exhibited a tough persona. But inside he was very troubled and had unusual fears for a man his age. She claimed that he slept with a flashlight because he was afraid of the dark.

"I feel Blake was planning Bonny's murder from the day after they got married . . ." her mother said. ". . . two days before my daughter died, she called me and told me something that chilled my heart." Bonny had allegedly told her of a major fight she'd had with Blake on May 2. Bonny's account indicated that Blake had suddenly turned on her without any apparent provocation.

"I've got a bullet with your name on it," Blake purportedly told Bonny during the fight.

"I'm not just some dumb country girl, you know," Bonny responded. "I must be kind of smart. I got you to finally marry me. I got myself a movie star and nobody thought I could do it."

"Girl, you better remember who you are fucking with," Blake supposedly said. "I'll kill your ass!"

Two days later Bonny Lee Bakley was dead.

Among the many things reported by Bonny's sister to the media after her death, was the existence of audiotapes that Bonny secretly had made of her telephone conversations with Blake and others. Margerry maintained that the tapes were a clear representation of the abusive relationship between Bonny and Blake. According to Margerry, Bonny told her family where she had hidden the tapes.

"These tapes are of intimate conversations with Bonny, Blake, and Christian Brando talking. Bonny told me these tapes would prove to the world that Blake was thinking about killing her constantly. She made the tapes in case anything should happen to her . . . I believe the tapes will answer a lot of questions that Blake doesn't want the police to know."

Robert Stefanow, a record producer who had been friends—and alleged sometime lover according to the *National Enquirer*—with Bonny for more than 16 years, told reporters and the police that Bonny had told him of Blake's attempts to kill her on two occasions.

"The first time was back in March or April of this year," Stefanow said. "Bonny told me they had gone on a weekend trip to a cabin he owns in the mountains. She said he slipped something into her drink to make her sleepy. She remembered being in bed beside him when Robert's bodyguard broke into the cabin waving a gun. The bodyguard stood over her pointing the gun as she woke up. Then she said he broke down in tears and said to Robert, 'I can't do it, boss. I can't do it.' "

Stefanow did not name the bodyguard. However, the next morning, according to Stefanow's recollection of what Bonny had purportedly told him, Blake told her that it would be in everyone's best interest if she legally signed over full custody of their daughter, Rose, to him.

Not long afterward, according to Stefanow, Bonny told him that Blake had offered $100,000 to her brother, Joey, to kill Bonny. After refusing the purported offer, Joey warned Bonny that she'd better watch her back.

CHAPTER 9

ROBERT BLAKE HAD LIVED A RELATIVELY QUIET LIFE at his Dilling Street home for the past 20 years. After making smart investments all those years, Blake managed to build an estimated net worth of $8.3 million, most of it riding on real estate. He did not have to work unless he wanted to, and when he wasn't showing up as a guest at the Playboy Mansion, where he liked to shoot pool, he could be seen doing the jitterbug at The Derby in Los Feliz or listening to jazz music at Jax in Glendale or at Lunaria in West LA. When he wasn't involved in those activities, he was known to drive off to the desert or into the mountains where he would be gone for days. Other favorite pastimes were attending to his gun collection or his collection of jazz recordings, or simply flirting with women. He was also known to spend many of his days reading, exercising, and going on three-hour lunches.

Blake is the type of man who never found it necessary to flaunt his celebrity status in order to keep his ego inflated. He was friendly to his neighbors, who described him as eccentric but sweet, and was helpful to them when the occasion called. He had few guests and, according to his son, Noah, didn't date much. But, said Noah, he loved to flirt with women much younger than himself. According to Noah, who had never met Bonny, Blake had a history of cutting off relationships with people that he had previously regarded highly for no apparent reason. Noah described his father as a "character," who could be affectionate but was often unavailable to others, including his own family.

"It was not uncommon for my dad and I to go long periods of time without talking," Noah said.

"He kinda kept to himself, but he was always nice to us," remarked a neighbor of Blake's.

There was a period when Blake made the rounds at the late-night talk shows, and he was a frequent guest on the *Tonight Show with Johnny Carson*, where he was popular for his outlandish behavior and irreverent remarks.

At the time of his made-for-television movie on killer John List, Blake showed up on a television talk show and made some chilling remarks, which seemed to have become a part of his routine.

"We're all in trouble," Blake said. "I'm 60 years old. I spent my life looking for the enemy. I sought out the enemy and found that he was me. I mean, there have been times I've had a gun on people. There's been times I've stalked somebody to kill him. Luckily enough, I never found him."

He once showed up on Roseanne Barr's talk show where he boasted that he could teach anyone to act. When the show's producers tried to get another appearance out of him to see if there was any substance to his claim, he declined, saying that he was no longer interested. With the passage of time and changing of hosts, the talk-show circuit dried up for him.

It was at his Dilling Street home where Blake met Earle Caldwell, an electronics installer and sometime handyman who had been sent there to install a car stereo for Blake. The two immediately hit it off, and before long Blake and Caldwell had become close friends and Caldwell found himself working as Blake's bodyguard. Although Caldwell was known to accompany Blake, and later Bonny as well, on trips, it was never confirmed publicly whether Caldwell was the same bodyguard who had purportedly accompanied them on the trip to the cabin in the mountains.

However, it was Caldwell who accompanied Bonny and Blake on their final vacation together when they went to Sequoia National Park on April 27, 2001, for a weekend getaway. They checked into a $240-per-night two-bedroom cottage at the Gateway Restaurant and Lodge, not far from the park. According to published reports, Caldwell stayed in one room while Bonny and Blake occupied the other. Blake reportedly slept on the queen-sized bed while Bonny slept on a cot. According to Gary Tomlin, a guide that Blake hired to take them into the park, the couple did not appear happy together.

"Robert totally ignored her, never held her hand, and insisted they sleep in separate beds at their motel," Tomlin said. "There would be total silence between them as they walked. He never touched her or did anything romantic."

When Tomlin took them into the park, one of their points of interest was Hospital Rock, which has steps that lead to the top. Following their stop at Hospital

Rock, their excursion went frighteningly awry, according to a county official.

"Mr. and Mrs. Blake, Caldwell, and a guide decided to climb Hospital Rock," reported Mike Davidson, battalion chief of the Tulare County Fire Department. "They all climbed the rock, which has 400 steps to the top, and then came down. But Mr. Caldwell decided he wanted to run to the top and down again. By the time he got back, he was feeling sick. And that night, back at the motel, he was short of breath, dizzy, had ringing in his ears and high blood pressure."

According to a bartender at the motel, Blake ran into the lounge shouting that his bodyguard had collapsed. The bartender said they called 911 for him. Paramedics checked him out a short time later and suspected that he was suffering from altitude sickness. To be on the safe side, the paramedics took him by ambulance down the mountain some 30 miles to a hospital, where he was treated and released a short time later.

"Robert wouldn't go," Tomlin said. "He said he was too tired and was going to bed. Bonny had to drive down the mountain herself . . . if Robert says he was so concerned about her safety that he had to carry a gun at all times, why did he make her drive alone at night down a dark winding road in his large van?"

Although Blake had originally reserved the cottage until April 30, they checked out a day early.

Blake's attorney, Harland Braun, and Earle Caldwell painted a different picture of Blake and Bonny's last outing together. When questions about the trip arose, Braun told the media that Blake and Bonny enjoyed each other's company that weekend, and Caldwell, in an appearance on the *Today* show, told Katie Couric a similar account of the trip.

"They were having fun," Caldwell said. "They were in the river, splashing around, swimming, having a good time."

Again there was a different portrayal of Blake and Bonny's relationship and their time spent together, and again it boiled down to who could be believed.

In the meantime stories began to surface about a mysterious man with a blond crew cut that had been seen lurking near Blake's home on several occasions, beginning a few weeks before Bonny's murder. Caldwell told the police and the media that Blake was worried that Bonny's lonely hearts business might be dangerous, and that was why he made the decision to hire Caldwell—for Bonny's protection.

"He always knew Bonny was in danger of being murdered," Caldwell said. "My job was to drive Bonny around and keep an eye out for anyone who might be following her. When we arrived somewhere, I had to check out the place first to make sure it was safe and then she could go in. She was always in fear of someone killing her . . . Bonny Lee ripped off so many men, it was inevitable that one of them would eventually come after her. I saw a letter on a table from some guy who was really ticked off at her. It said something like, 'I'm going to get you for what you did to me.' "

According to Braun, one letter dated March 12 was found in her belongings that were turned over to the police. It was from a man boasting that he had taken a hit out on his ex-wife's boyfriend. The man claimed that he had been subjected to extortion attempts, and he told Bonny: "Don't even bother if that's your motive." Many of the men that Bonny had scammed were violent, Braun contended.

"She once told me," Caldwell said, "I have an old boyfriend in New Jersey who's so infatuated with me, he says if he can't have me, no one can.' "

According to Caldwell, Blake tried very hard to persuade Bonny to give up her scams. He even provided her with a $10,000-a-month allowance in the hope that would convince her to stop.

"But whatever amount Robert gave her," Caldwell said, "it was never enough. Scamming was in her blood. It gave her a thrill to rip people off. Even when the men wrote angry letters, she continued."

According to what Caldwell told the police, he first saw the man watching Blake's house less than two months before Bonny's murder, which would have been around March. He said that the man would often sit in a black four-door pickup parked on the street and stare at Blake's residence. After a while, he said, Blake became so concerned that he sent the baby to stay with his relatives in Calabasas.

"I was the first to see the guy," Caldwell said. "I named him Buzz Cut."

On one occasion, Caldwell said, Buzz Cut arrived

Actor Robert Blake. *(AP/Wide World Photo)*

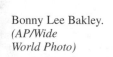

Bonny Lee Bakley. *(AP/Wide World Photo)*

Legendary rock star Jerry Lee Lewis, with whom Bakley claimed to have had a daughter. *(AP/Wide World Photo)*

"Mata Hari"—Blake's home in Los Angeles' Studio City district. *(AP/Wide World Photo)*

This smaller house at the back of Blake's Studio City property is where Bakley lived with her daughter during her marriage to Blake. *(AP/Wide World Photo)*

Vitello's Italian Restaurant, outside of which Bonny Lee Bakley was shot in the head, has gained a level of notoriety since the murder. Here an anonymous onlooker waits near the spot where Bakley was killed. *(AP/Wide World Photo)*

Los Angeles Police Detective Dan Jenks walks past the spot where Bonny Lee Bakley was murdered while sitting in Robert Blake's 1991 Dodge Stealth. *(AP/Wide World Photo)*

Defense attorney Barry Levin at the crime scene. Nearby is a shrine set up in memory of Bonny Lee Bakley that includes a Mother's Day card signed by the victim's children. *(AP/Wide World Photo)*

Right: Los Angeles Police Detective Juan Parga, seen here investigating the construction site adjacent to where Bakley was murdered. *(AP/Wide World Photo)*

Left: LAPD detectives search through material taken from Blake's home. *(AP/Wide World Photo)*

Below: Defense attorney Harland Braun speaks to reporters at police headquarters on Thursday, May 10. *(AP/Wide World Photo)*

Earle Caldwell, Robert Blake's bodyguard. *(AP/Wide World Photo)*

Filmmaker Sean Stanek, who placed the 911 call following Bakley's murder. *(AP/Wide World Photo)*

During a Monday, May 14 news conference, LAPD Commander Garrett Zimmon tells the media that authorities have no suspects in the killing. *(AP/Wide World Photo)*

Sondra Kerr Blake, Blake's former wife, at a June 1 news conference. *(AP/Wide World Photo)*

Pallbearers carry the body of Bonny Lee Bakley to her grave during a ceremony in Los Angeles on Friday, May 25. *(AP/Wide World Photo)*

Robert Blake places a hand on his wife's coffin. *(AP/Wide World Photo)*

Blake holds Rose Lenore Sophie Blake, the daughter he had with Bonny Lee Bakley, following Bakley's burial. *(AP/Wide World Photo)*

in the middle of the night, parked his truck, and turned the lights off. He sneered and drove away as Blake approached him and shined a flashlight in his face. That hadn't kept him from coming back, however. He returned repeatedly over a month-long period, and on one occasion Caldwell and Blake chased him through the neighborhood, to no avail. Caldwell described the man as thin, in his twenties, and probably about five feet eight inches tall.

Caldwell's interview with the police lasted approximately two hours and, like everything else associated with the investigation of Bonny's murder, the police had little to say about what Caldwell told them. Most of the details of the interview came from Caldwell himself, and there were no definitive explanations offered about not getting the license plate number of the pickup Buzz Cut had been driving so that they could report it to the police. Caldwell did say that when the interview was over, he came away feeling that the homicide detectives were only looking at Blake as a suspect in Bonny's murder. It appeared to Caldwell that the police were being rigid in that they did not seem to be considering other evidence.

"It was clear to me they weren't looking for anything different," Caldwell said. "They have their minds set. I'm sure they think Robert did it."

"It's unfortunate that he feels that way," LAPD Lieutenant Horace Frank said. "Certainly we're not in a position to dictate how he feels. The investigation is going to be a painstaking process involving many different interviews."

"We want them to investigate Blake—we're not trying to hide anything—and every other possible suspect . . ." Braun reiterated. "All I know is I stood there and told them what to search for. I explained to them what her business was [and that] her letters would be an indication of who would have an inclination to kill her."

"The department is conducting a full investigation in this matter," Frank said, explaining that the detectives were examining all pertinent and legitimate evidence associated with the case. "They only took what would assist them in solving this particular crime," he said, referring to items removed during the searches of Blake's home.

"Robert is very distraught that the police aren't looking into Bonny Lee's past for clues to the killer," Caldwell said. "He isn't worried about being arrested because he knows he didn't do it. But he's concerned that the real killer will never be found . . . I know for a fact that Robert didn't kill Bonny Lee Bakley. The killer was a guy who had been following her for some time and finally moved in at an opportune moment, when no one was around, so Robert would look like the guilty party . . ."

Caldwell also provided some insight into Blake and Bonny's lifestyle, as well as the fear he said Blake had for his wife's safety.

"Their schedules are a lot different," he said. "She's a night person, and he's an early-morning kind of guy . . . he told me many times, 'I'm 67 years old, I got this beautiful baby, I'll do anything. We'll get this [marriage] to work . . .' " But Blake worried. "He was getting weird phone calls, and there were people kind of hanging out by the house who clearly weren't neighborhood kids."

CHAPTER 10

HARLAND W. BRAUN, 58, SEEMED LIKE HE WAS ON the scene within minutes after Bonny Lee Bakley's murder, and was nearly as quick to step in front of news media to begin exposing the victim's character in a controversial tactic recognized in legal circles as "dirtying the victim." Blake, according to many legal analysts, had made a wise choice in deciding to bring the UCLA law school graduate on board as his attorney. Braun, who called the prosecutors in the Rampart police scandal trial "pond scum," is known throughout Los Angeles legal circles for his outspokenness and tenacity, but perhaps more so for his unpredictability. When confronted about his controversial methods regarding Bakley's past, he smiled and said that he was just doing his job by informing the police, as well as the public, that many people might have had a motive to kill his client's wife besides Blake.

Despite his controversial methods, many of Braun's colleagues portrayed him as a brilliant attorney who would stop at nothing—as long as his actions remain legal and ethical—to help his clients.

"He has no fear, and that is his greatest asset," said attorney Mark Geragos, who has tried about fifty cases with Braun. "He's not afraid to humiliate himself," if it means helping his client.

Braun, born to a registered nurse and a Los Angeles

cattle-hide dealer, began his legal career during the "free love" movement in 1968 when he went to work for the Los Angeles County District Attorney's office as a deputy prosecutor. He described his job with the DA's office as working for the "dark side," and only endured the position for five years. He decided to go over to the "other side" because he wasn't fond of trying to put people in jail. He also made the move to practicing criminal law because of a major distrust of the criminal-justice system.

"The way I look at it is," Braun said, "going to work every day in the criminal system is like going to a mental institution. I regard it as totally irrational and immoral."

Braun represented a number of high-profile clients over the years, including a police officer in the Rodney King police-brutality case, and movie director John Landis and four others in the *Twilight Zone: The Movie* case (Landis and his producer were charged with involuntary manslaughter in the helicopter crash deaths of actor Vic Morrow and several small children). Braun and Deputy District Attorney Lea Purwin D'Agostino went several verbal rounds during the trial in which Braun, at one point, called D'Agostino "scum." She retorted that it would not be beneath Braun to call his own mother a liar if he thought it would help him get his clients off. All five of the defendants were acquitted of the charges.

"Harland speaks in sound bites," D'Agostino recently said. "He is a master at it. Because of that, people don't realize that he is also extraordinarily bright and is very knowledgeable." Despite the fact that she and Braun are friends, D'Agostino doesn't condone his tactics, particularly with the Bakley case. "I don't believe the victim should be put on trial," she said.

Cary Goldstein, the Bakley family's attorney, apparently agreed.

"I feel like she's being treated as the defendant," Goldstein said. "The spin on this matter by Mr. Blake and his counsel is a disgrace."

By Braun's own accounting, his career as a criminal defense lawyer didn't really take off until he defended Vincent Bugliosi in 1974. Bugliosi, who had led the prosecution in the Charles Manson murder trial, was accused of leaking a document to a news reporter and later lying about it while under oath after leaving the district attorney's office and entering private practice. He was indicted on suspicion of perjury, but Braun got the indictment dismissed.

"Even though it was a bogus case," Braun said, "the public learned that I got it dismissed and decided that I must be good."

During the Rodney King trial, Braun clashed with everyone from the prosecutor to the judge to his fellow defense attorneys. Right before jury selection was set to begin, Braun publicly stated that he felt it could be difficult to find impartial African-Americans to sit on the jury. One of his colleagues accused him of being irresponsible and offensive, and warned that his statement might have had a negative influence on any African-Americans chosen as jurors.

"Harland knows when to capitalize on a weakness," remarked attorney Barry Levin, who worked with

Braun on the Rampart scandal case. "And he knows when to explore a strength in his own case." Levin, who joined Braun on Blake's team on May 12, agreed with the tactics Braun was using in the Blake situation and said that even though it might not be the popular thing to do, it was necessary. "Harland recognizes whatever is put out there first, sticks. I think he is doing a masterful job at controlling bad publicity for his client in this case."

Braun told reporters that he chose Levin to join the case not only because he had worked with him in the past but because he represented police officers and was a former police officer himself.

"If you're not guilty, you want to be exonerated, and the only way you can be exonerated is to make sure the police investigation is done properly," Braun commented.

Levin echoed Braun's comments as he toured the crime scene and walked past the now-dried flowers that had been placed on the utility box near where Bonny was killed. Bonny's grown children, it was learned, had placed some of the flowers there.

"I want the police to do a thorough and complete job," Levin said.

"I love the guy," said private investigator Scott Ross of Braun, who was working for him on the Bakley case. "But Harland straddles between pure genius and completely insane."

There were concerns being aired throughout the Los Angeles legal community that, if a suspect in Bonny Lee Bakley's murder was identified and brought to trial, Braun's tactics regarding his "dirtying the victim" in such an aggressive public manner might serve to taint any potential jury pools. Nonetheless, it didn't stop him.

Braun was soon telling reporters that his investigators had turned up numerous ex-husbands of Bonny's, and he stated that he believed that she might have been married as many as 100 times.

"The question is whether she ever got divorced," Braun said.

As one day followed another, the print, television, and radio news media continued digging up dirt on Bonny's past. Once the frenzy began, the media did not need much help from either of Blake's lawyers. They began running the content of many of Bonny's ads that had first appeared in adult magazines such as *Sun, TS Contact,* and *Kinky,* and they managed to get ahold of many of the letters that Bonny had written to her marks. She also placed ads in the personals columns of a number of newspapers.

"Hi Single Guy," began one letter. "Pretty, still single gal wants to get to know you." She called herself Miss Lee Bakley, and wrote that her measurements were 38-27-38, and stated that she had recently lost her job at a car wash but had obtained a part-time job stocking grocery store shelves. "Yuk! I do hate it . . . Can you, will you save me from this horrible fate?" She even suggested moving in with her "Single Guy" for a while, and asked that he send enough cash for a motel room and gas. The suggested amount was $200, but if he could only send $20 she would mail him her "sexiest pictures" as well as a tape of her singing.

"Men wanted—any age from anywhere," read one of Bonny's ads that appeared in an adult magazine and was accompanied by a nude photo of Bonny in a provocative pose.

"I'm sad and lonely due to a recent breakup," read another ad. "Looks are unimportant . . . I do love older men mostly!" It was signed, "Miss Bonny Bakley."

Another one read: "Don't just look! You can touch me. All I need is $30 in gas money and I can be at your side."

One letter found inside Blake's home after Bonny was killed, which was among those copied and released by Braun included the following: "I don't have anyone to spend the holidays with, do you? My family lives too far away, could I spend them with you?" It was signed "Miss Leebonny Bakley." Many of the letters sent to the men who responded to her adult-magazine ads were form letters, and nearly all of them echoed a similar down-on-her-luck story.

Many of the photos of Bonny were raunchy. Some depicted her nearly totally naked, while others showed her fondling herself. Braun believes that her photos likely played a part in getting her killed.

"Her past may have come back to haunt her," Braun said. "This seems to be a revenge killing. Robert did a background check on her and found a criminal history of taking out want ads to bilk lonely old men out of money. He warned her to give it up and she said she would, but apparently she was still doing it. She was the mother of his child, and that's why he married her. But I guess her con schemes caught up with Bonny Lee and there were a number of people who had it in for her."

Instead of giving up her scams, Braun said, she rented a mailbox for her businesses in Studio City on April 6, 2001. During the investigation into her murder, LAPD detectives obtained the contents of the mailbox. There were numerous letters from various men, and some of the envelopes had money stuffed inside. She was still going under a number of different names, and it seemed very likely that she was still using phony identification and had done so to rent the mailbox. The detectives learned that in at least one instance regarding the Studio City mailbox, Bonny had gone under the identification of a friend who claimed that several key pieces of her identification had somehow disappeared.

After Bonny began taping her telephone conversations with others, a tape surfaced in which she openly talked about her criminal convictions for using multiple identities. She also talked about her scams without shame.

"Yeah, I got three years probation just for having different IDs, you know," she said on the tape, chatting casually with a friend. "And it wasn't even like I was using them for anything totally illegal, either. I mean, it's my business and if I want to, like fool guys and say that I'm somebody else, what's the difference?"

According to one of her family members, Bonny felt no shame or guilt about bilking her victims out of money.

"She would place an ad in a swingers' magazine saying she was lonely and couldn't find the right guy to give her what she wanted and asking men to write," explained a family member whose identity wasn't revealed. "Then she'd reply to their letters saying she'd be on their doorstep within days if only she had money for gas. She'd enclose her picture with her legs wide open and boobs exposed. Sometimes there would be a caption with the words, 'Why just look when you can touch?' When she received the money, she'd write again, saying that her car had conked out and she needed $50 for repairs. The ruse went on and on. Then she'd need new tires or a plane ticket. Eventually the mark would get the message and stop sending money. Bonny had no remorse. She said any guy stupid enough to send her money deserved to be taken."

In many of her letters to her marks, Bonny would typically ask for $75 or a plane ticket but would add: "If you can't afford this, please send me a Christmas gift and a $10 or $20 bill to help me out. I'll send you some nudie shots of me, of course, in my next letter."

In the meantime, as the investigation continued, it was revealed that the police were focusing on two different theories, according to an unnamed inside source that talked to the media.

According to the *Enquirer*, a source told them that "Blake has become a full-blown suspect. They want to know why he parked around the corner from the restaurant on the night of the murder and then left

Bonny alone even though he was so concerned about her being killed he'd gotten a concealed weapons permit. Also, the window on Bonny's side of the car was down, not broken. She wasn't scared and no one heard a scream, either. The [investigators] say Blake wanted custody of their child and that Bonny had threatened Robert, saying she would take the baby away from him.

"The police are also looking at a man who made threats against Blake's wife," continued the source. "That man claims that Bonny bilked his father out of all his money. The man supposedly told her, 'You're married to a movie star now, and you need to pay me back.' He threatened to harm her to get the money and police took tapes from the Blake house documenting the threats from the other man."

Blake's maid, Lydia Benavides, also told the police about Blake's fear for his wife's safety.

"He always says, 'Keep the gate locked,' and that's what I do," Benavides said. "I know he was afraid of something, because he says, 'Keep the gate closed. Don't leave it open.' "

In a 1993 interview with *People* magazine, Blake provided some of his own insight into the mind of a killer.

"A murderer only becomes a murderer after he or she kills somebody," Blake said. "But what are they before they're on Death Row? They're you or me."

CHAPTER 11

AS THE LAPD'S INVESTIGATION INTO BONNY LEE Bakley's mysterious murder continued, so did attorney Harland Braun's media spin. He appeared intent on fully exposing the details of her shady past in an effort to keep the detectives looking for possible suspects from her past and away from his client, Robert Blake. The Los Angeles police officers, as well as the prosecutors in the district attorney's office, were also well aware that their every move would be placed under public scrutiny, which is typical in most crimes that involve celebrities. They had to move slowly in order to match wits with such high-profile, as well as high-priced, criminal defense attorneys like Braun and Levin. And in order to accomplish that not-so-easy task, they had to have all of their ducks in order, so to speak. There could be no room for mistakes in this case, and it was necessary that they distance themselves as far as possible from the so-called court of public opinion that, along with the news media and supermarket tabloids, had all but convicted Robert Blake of murdering his wife. If they participated in the three-ring circus and their investigation, or Blake's own investigation for that matter, turned up a suspect around whom an iron-case could be built, it would be an embarrassment from which they would find it difficult, if not impossible, to recover. Even though it is normal, and even necessary, for the police to focus on the spouse of a murder victim in their investigation, it was Braun's and Levin's job to ensure that they looked at all of the possibilities.

"There is incredible pressure," said Deputy Los Angeles District Attorney Lea Purwin D'Agostino, in such cases involving celebrities. "Everyone is going to microscopically examine everything you have done . . . You know that people are going to be second-guessing—'Are they [celebrities] going to be getting special treatment?' "

As a case in point, D'Agostino cited the 1984 federal prosecution of former automaker John DeLorean, who had been charged with drug trafficking. In DeLorean's case, the prosecution lost because De-Lorean's lawyers had done in essence what Blake's lawyers have been doing, namely creating a battle of sorts in the court of public opinion. The O. J. Simpson case is yet another good example of the aforementioned, in which the LAPD as well as the district attorney's office made a feverish "rush to judgment," ending with Simpson's ultimate acquittal.

While the LAPD and the Los Angeles District Attorney's Office contend that celebrity cases do not get more attention than any other case, they do, according to former Los Angeles District Attorney Ira Reiner. The police are working with a double-edged sword when they investigate a celebrity case. On the one hand they do everything that they can to avoid giving the impression that they give more attention to a celebrity case than other cases, and on the other hand they have to worry about being placed in the hot seat inside the courtroom and accused of handling a less-than-perfect investigation. Celebrity cases, said Reiner, are also reviewed at a higher level at the district attorney's office than are cases involving noncelebrities.

"It's just not going to be handled routinely," Reiner said. Celebrities are in fact given special treatment, he said. "But it's not the kind that anyone would want. You get a dozen detectives assigned to it full time who are told to get to it right now. Everyone gives it special attention. You are not getting a break."

A good example of Reiner's assessment can be seen in the Bonny Bakley murder. The captain as well as the lieutenant of the LAPD Robbery-Homicide Division, as well as the lead deputy prosecutor of the Major Crimes Division of the district attorney's office, visited the Bakley crime scene, a duty which is normally handed off to those lower on the police and district attorney's office hierarchy.

Reiner has experienced first-hand the difficulties of such high-profile cases. He lost the McMartin preschool molestation case that dragged on for months and was essentially tried in the public before it ever made it into the courtroom. He also lost the first Menendez brothers murder trial—that trial ended in a hung jury. The case resulted in convictions the next time around. Many in Los Angeles legal circles contend that it was those losses that caused Reiner to lose the election in 1992 to Gil Garcetti, who faced a similar downfall with the O. J. Simpson case that, some say, resulted in him losing his office to Steve Cooley in 2000. Now Cooley, trying to learn from the lessons of his predecessors and avoid their fate, is handling the Blake case, his first celebrity case (Robert Downey Jr.'s legal woes not withstanding), with kid gloves.

In 1997, when Bill Cosby's son, Ennis, was murdered, Mayor Richard Riordan told the public that the case would be given top priority, only to be corrected by Willie L. Williams, the LAPD's chief at the time, who promptly came out and said that the Cosby case would be treated equally to all of the other cases they were investigating. Now Cooley's office insists that all the cases his office prosecutes are handled fairly and equally, and that it is the complexity of the case and not the celebrity involved that determines the level of treatment afforded them.

"We handle them professionally and give them all the attention they deserve," said Sandi Gibbons, spokeswoman for the Los Angeles County District Attorney's Office. The police working the Bakley investigation agree.

"We understand the fact that people might perceive that more than usual resources are devoted to high-profile crimes," said Captain James Tatreau, who is leading the Bakley murder investigation. "But some of that is generated by the media exposure and the leads that they generate. Those have to be dealt with. If not, an accused person has a possible legitimate claim that there were things that were not pursued."

Tatreau and his colleagues were determined that was not going to be the situation with the Bakley case, and argued that nine detectives sent out to the crime scene the next morning was not all that unusual. It allowed them, he said, to spread out and canvass the neighborhood in their search for clues as well as potential witnesses before the crime scene became contaminated and witnesses tainted by media reports.

"You want to do it before the media does," Tatreau said.

"It used to be just whodunit," said LAPD spokesman Sergeant John Pasquariello. "But we realize the attention's going to be on us as much as it's going to be on the crime itself. We've got to be cognizant of that, and realize we're under the same light as everybody else in this scene. We've got to be particular about how our image is portrayed."

Image had suddenly become all-important to the LAPD, particularly after the Simpson trial and the bad-taste left by detective Mark Fuhrman's perjury about making racist comments, which only served to help Simpson's defense.

"There was a little intimidation factor [in the Simpson case]," Fuhrman told *The Los Angeles Times*. It was like, " 'Oh my God, we have to arrest O. J. Simpson.' Well, so what?"

Fuhrman told the newspaper that the LAPD has learned lessons from the Simpson case, particularly about not being overly sensitive when a celebrity is involved. Fuhrman contended that it was Simpson's status as a celebrity that caused the LAPD to make mistakes, like putting off arresting Simpson even though they had amassed sufficient evidence to do so.

"I think the thing they've learned is, you do it the same way as always," Fuhrman said. "You don't make special considerations, special options, nothing."

Have lessons actually been learned since the Simpson case? And have they been applied to the Blake-Bakley case? Attorney Carl E. Douglas, who served as one of Simpson's attorneys, thinks they have, particularly about moving too quickly.

"The police were justifiably criticized years ago for rushing to judgment," Douglas said. "Certainly each case is different. But I think they were particularly mindful to characterize Blake as simply a witness and not a suspect."

"The district attorney's office makes the biggest push to show that they handle all cases with care," said civil-rights attorney Leo J. Terrell, who disagrees that all cases are handled equally. "But the truth of the matter is that more attention is given to [celebrity] cases because of the political motivations of the district attorney's office." Such political motivations can be traced back historically, when favors were done in years gone by for the movie industry, a mainstay of Southern California life and a very major employer.

"Everything is scrutinized and reevaluated," Terrell said. "Prosecutors try to give the impression that this is how the system works in all cases."

Of course, the prosecutors and the police in Bakley's case have no control over how Blake's attorney, Harland Braun, is portraying her in the media spotlight. With his portrayal of Bakley as a grifter, star stalker, and con artist who used promises of sex to swindle men through her lonely hearts ads in newspapers and adult magazines, his characterization of her made news across the country and could ultimately affect the outcome of the case. Even by her own family's admissions, however, it all seemed to be true, making it difficult to make an argument against his tactics that could either point the police in the right direction or lead them down a trail of false leads and waste valuable time.

"She's been involved in these kind of con schemes where you bilk lonely men out of money with ads across the country," Braun said. "So there could be any number of people that would have had it in for her."

At least one person, however, was of the opinion that Braun went too far: Johnnie Cochran, the attorney who helped get O. J. Simpson's acquittal. "Braun's an excellent lawyer," Cochran told CNN. "I'm a little bit amazed, though, even for Harland, the way he's attacked the victim, who's not even buried. I mean, he's attacking her, releasing stuff about her. It's almost like, 'Thou protest too much.' And it's a very strange case. Only in Hollywood . . . but . . . he's an excellent lawyer."

Gloria Allred, another high-profile attorney who represented Blake's ex-wife, Sondra Kerr, conceded Braun's talent as an attorney. However, the feminist lawyer recently said that she thinks Braun's strategy of "dirtying the victim" was outrageous.

"It's one of the worst [examples of dirtying the victim]," Allred said, "because I have to believe as an attorney that Mr. Braun would not do this unless he were authorized by his client to do it. So that means

Mr. Blake is in the process through his agent, namely his attorney, of smearing the mother of his child, a murder victim . . . I think it's going to have a different impact than it might have pre-O. J. Simpson, when Nicole Brown Simpson was trashed. People are a little more sophisticated now, especially LA County Superior Court juries are a little bit more sophisticated about defense tactics, and the attack on the mother of Mr. Blake's child I don't think is going to go over very well. I mean, whatever she did, she didn't deserve to be murdered."

"I certainly know Harland Braun very well, and he's a *very* bright man and a brilliant attorney, and if I were in trouble I'd certainly want someone like Braun on my side," said Deputy District Attorney D'Agostino. "But you know, do I agree with his policy of attacking a victim and smearing a victim? Absolutely not. But this is something, there's an adage: The best defense is a good offense, and that's what he's doing."

Others, like UC-Berkeley's law school professor Charles Weisselberg, believed that Braun's efforts were the result of a strategy aimed at removing some of the pressure off the district attorney's office, which could serve to keep Blake from being swiftly arrested.

"He may be doing it because this is a high-profile case and he wants to take some heat off the district attorney, who may be feeling some pressure to go at Mr. Blake," Weisselberg said. "In other words, you've got an elected district attorney in Los Angeles, and an elected district attorney doesn't want the public to feel that he's soft on somebody because of their celebrity status, and this tactic may in part make it easier for the district attorney to go slow with Mr. Blake." In other words, by diminishing sympathy for the victim, he is weakening the demand for a speedy resolution of the case.

"There's intense press coverage, obviously," D'Agostino said. "And actually that hurts the prosecution in many cases. The media, the tabloids, for example, go and seek out witnesses, they interview them and they pay them before they can even testify, which of course destroys them as witnesses for the prosecution, and sometimes precludes us from even being able to call them as witnesses . . . you know that everything you do is going to be analyzed and second-guessed [when a celebrity case goes to trial]. As a prosecutor, if you stop and think about it, it isn't a heck of a lot of fun working under the conditions of being second-guessed by, you know, sometimes panels of experts on the boob tube, mostly experts from New York who don't know California law. And if they do know California law, the bottom line is that none of these experts really knows your case . . . We don't have royalty in America, and movie stars have become our royalty, and it's very difficult. People are very startruck. Let's not mince words about it, they are, and that makes it hard . . . I think Harland knows exactly what he's doing. I think because a lot of the comments that he makes are so off the wall, people don't realize how bright he is, and I sometimes think perhaps he does that to mask the brilliance."

"With a high-profile defendant, one who doesn't have a criminal record, it seems like the jury really is able to afford the person the presumption of innocence," said Weisselberg, who agrees with D'Agostino's assessment. "And there are many people in the criminal justice system who think that folks with prior criminal records or people represented in run-of-the-mill cases are not looked at the same way by the jury. There's just so much more going on" in high-profile cases, he said.

Those critical of Braun's tactics say that he tainted potential jury pools with the intense pretrial publicity created in the Bakley case. Some said that such publicity could necessitate a change of venue if the case went to trial regardless of who was eventually charged in Bakley's murder. However, Professor Weisselberg didn't see a change of venue as being much of an issue.

"A typical case with a change of venue might be a high-profile homicide case in a relatively modest-sized county, where lots of people in the county knew the victim, or everybody followed the case," Weisselberg said. "It's hard for me to imagine that the level of publicity thus far in the Blake case has tainted a jury in a county the size of Los Angeles to the degree that a fair trial can't be found here. That's kind of hard for me to imagine."

Attorney Gloria Allred, however, wasn't so sure that an impartial jury could be found to judge such a case.

"They do say that they will only judge a case by the admissible evidence that's presented in a court of law and will remain fair and impartial and try to set aside whatever they've learned outside of the court of law," Allred said. "Having said that, [juries] are human beings, and it's hard to unring a bell once it's been rung. If you've seen an elephant in a room and someone says, 'Forget that you've seen that elephant in the room,' it may be difficult."

D'Agostino agreed with Allred's assessment that high-intensity publicity could damage a prosecutor's case, and used as an example a scene from the Susan Hayward movie, *Heat of Anger*, in which Hayward portrayed a defense attorney representing a so-called high-profile client.

"She's in front of a jury," D'Agostino said, describing the scene from the movie, "and I just always think of this particular line. There was this incredible amount of publicity on that particular case, and she tells all the jurors to close their eyes, and she stands in front of them as only this beautiful Susan Hayward could do, and she says, 'Now I want you to think of anything in the world that you want to think about except a blue horse. Whatever you do, do not think of a blue horse. What*ever* you do, do not think of a blue horse.' And then she pauses for a while—of course you can't do this in court—and she says, 'Open your eyes,' and she looked at them and she started smiling and she says, 'And of course, that's all any of you could think of was the blue horse because I told you not to.' . . . Harland really is an excellent attorney. He truly is."

That illustration could very well fit into the Bakley

murder case. Who on a jury would be able to forget everything they heard about the case?

"I think it cuts both ways," said criminal defense attorney Gerald L. Chaleff, who also represented the Menendez brothers during their first trial for killing their millionaire parents. "It puts added pressure on both sides.

CHAPTER 12

A DARK CLOUD HUNG OVER THE HEADS OF MANY OF
Hal Roach's *Our Gang* and *Little Rascals* actors for
many years, prompting some to contend that the misery of their later years and, ultimately, the untimely
deaths of many of them, was the result of a curse or
hex that had been placed on them by person or per-
sons unknown. But to believe that, one would have to
be of the same mentality exhibited by the *Our Gang*
personalities themselves while in full character! Curse
or no curse, many of them were troubled and some
of them merely the victims of pure bad luck.

Carl Switzer, who played Alfalfa, was shot to death
at age 31; William Thomas, who played Buckwheat,
died at age 49 of a heart attack; Darla Hood, who
played Darla, came down with hepatitis and died at
age 47; Kendall McComas, who played Breezy Bris-
bane, committed suicide at 64; William Robert
Laughlin, who played Froggy, was killed in a motor-
scooter accident when he was 16; Norman Chaney,
who played Chubby, died following surgery at age 22;
Matthew Bear, who played Stymie, was a criminal
and a drug addict who died of a stroke at 56; Scotty
Beckett, who played Scotty, died of an apparent over-
dose of barbiturates at age 38; Robert Hutchins, who
played Wheezer, was killed in a military airplane accident at 19; even Pete the Pup was poisoned by an

unknown person, but one of Pete's offspring was able to take over the role.

Robert Blake, of course, who played Mickey in the comedy series, was the latest of the *Our Gang* kids-turned-adult to have the spotlight of scandal and misery aimed at him. Although he had the dark cloud of the so-called "curse" hanging over his head for much of his troubled life, his troubles only grew deeper when police began looking at him as a suspect in Bonny's murder. Now that he's entered the third act of his life, the current stream of publicity has created a stigma that he might find difficult to shake—unless the police quickly identified a suspect other than Blake to focus on, a suspect who would be charged and convicted.

Some dubbed Blake's current situation as "O. J.: The Sequel," the story of an actor in the autumn of his years thrust into a media frenzy centering on sex, scams, paternity questions, and the death of a wife of ill repute that he might not have wanted to live out his final years with anyway. Blake likely would rather have passed a role like that on to another actor.

Marcia Clark, who played a major role as one of the prosecutors in the O. J. case even came forward with her opinion in this case. When she was recently asked who had killed Bonny Bakley, she responded, "I think he [Blake] did!" She believed that Braun's tactics were going to hurt Blake in the long run.

"Smearing the victim is not a good idea," Clark said. "I think it's going to be detrimental to Blake.

It's going to wind up generating sympathy for Bakley. It looks desperate. It's making Blake look guilty and afraid. And, remember, he's no gem."

In the meantime, the detectives working on the case kept asking themselves the same, gnawing questions that they had raised at the outset of the case. Why did Blake make a reservation at Vitello's when he hadn't in the past? Since he had been coming there for over 20 years three or four times a week, they would have gladly accommodated him on the night in question without one. Why did he park in a secluded area a block and a half away, beneath a burned-out street-light? Why hadn't he parked instead in Vitello's parking lot, which was well lighted with people coming and going on a somewhat regular basis?

They didn't have the answers to those questions, and it appeared doubtful that they ever would. There could have been any number of reasons why Blake made the decisions he did that night, none of which would mean that he had killed Bonny. They also considered the theory that Blake might have murdered Bonny at another location before transporting her body back there. But again, there was no evidence at this point to support such a theory.

And what about Bonny? If everything that Braun was saying about her was true, why wouldn't it be possible, even plausible, that someone out of her past had done her in for revenge? She was, after all, no Mother Teresa. She had lived a rather pathetic, even despicable life as a parasite living off of the success of others, not to mention her illegal scamming activities. Her victims ranged into the thousands. By some accounts as many as 25,000 men had fallen prey to her in one way or another. So why couldn't someone she had screwed have gone after her? Her attitude about her activities can best be summed up by her own words: "I think psychologically it helps me get even with mankind. My father tried to get fresh with me when I was seven, while my mother was in the hospital having Joey. He died before I could grow up and kill him."

And then there was Blake's last role as Mystery Man in David Lynch's dark, eerily disturbing picture, *Lost Highway*. As the movie's villain, Blake looked the part with his greased-back hair and ghostly white makeup that contrasted with his black suit and dark, deep-set eyes. Blake's part called for him to torment the main character, a musician who played the saxophone, by apparently showing up in two places simultaneously. Blake can play a psychotic character like no other. In *In Cold Blood*, he delivered one the film's best lines when his character, Perry Smith, said, "I despise people who can't control themselves." Blake was at his best in such roles because he made them believable. One wonders how he was able to deliver such stunning performances without being unbalanced himself.

Even the comparisons between *Lost Highway* and Bonny Bakley's murder were chilling. In the film, a musician suspects his wife of being unfaithful and he ultimately murders her. The musician is also being watched by a stalker, who provides him with video-tapes that show how he had been loitering outside the house, watching him. Blake's bodyguard, Earle Cald-well, noticed the man he eventually named Buzz Cut watching Blake's house in the weeks before Bonny's murder; the similarity was almost frightening. But it was, after all, just a movie, and it could have no bear-ing on the case being investigated. Or could it?

In postulating theories that someone out of Bonny's past may have killed her, the police had to look carefully at the impressive estate she left behind from her mostly illegal activities. She did, after all, own more than $500,000 in real estate at the time of her death. One house in Memphis, purchased in 1988 for $73,710, was now valued at $86,200. She pur-chased another house in Memphis in 1991 for $69,587 that was now worth $80,800. She also bought two undeveloped lots in Memphis in 1995, one for $62,790 and the other for $137,623. And then, in 1998, she bought an 11,000-square-foot house in Thousand Oaks, California, for $185,000 that was now valued at $275,000 to $300,000. Not bad for ripping off lonely old men.

The house in Thousand Oaks, investigators learned, was a rental, both when she purchased it and at the present time. The current tenant, Joanne Fenton, who has resided there with her husband and two adult step-children for the past eight years, was able to provide a little insight into Bakley's demeanor a few weeks before her murder.

Fenton had seen her landlord only twice, the first

time being just prior to Bakley's purchase of the
house, and the second time approximately five or six
weeks before her murder when she showed up at the
house with Blake. According to Fenton, Bonny looked
markedly different from the first time that she had
seen her. Her hair was somewhat shorter and she had
lost considerable weight, and didn't really seem like
herself.

"She seemed nervous, scattered, a bit strange,"
Fenton said. "And she had this little-girl voice going
on." She said that Bakley introduced Blake as her
boyfriend and not her husband. Blake, who was
dressed in black, never corrected her regarding their
relationship. Fenton said that Bonny seemed intimidated by Blake, who was not particularly friendly.

"He was very businesslike," Fenton said. "They did
not look like a happy couple. There was definitely no
love connection there. They seemed like two people
who were there to do a business deal. No warmth or
affection between them. That's the last time we heard
from her."

As the investigators continued to probe into
Bonny's financial affairs, they learned that she had
made enough money to loan her half brother, Peter
Carlyon, and his friend, Jerry Spencer, enough for
them to start their own landscaping business in Memphis. Spencer was not surprised, he said, when he
learned that Bonny had been murdered. He said that
she had expressed to him her fear of both Blake and
Christian Brando.

"I would talk to her regularly," Spencer said, "and
she would say things were getting bad," referring to

the relationship between Bonny and Blake. "She said, 'If anything ever happens to me, it will be because of him.'" Spencer said that Bonny was also afraid of Brando.

"He had already killed someone," Spencer said, "so she was worried that he might do something to her . . . I know there were others who were angry at her, but I think they are miniscule compared to her concerns about Blake and Brando."

While examining Bonny's personal papers and belongings authorities came across information related to a life insurance policy in the amount of $400,000 on which Bonny was paying premiums. The policy was listed on the prenuptial agreement that Blake had put together but which was never signed, and it listed Bonny as the beneficiary but said nothing regarding the name of the insured.

Braun said that he suspected the insurance policy might have been taken out on Blake, which caused him some concern because she had not revealed in her papers who was named on the policy. In order to take out a life insurance policy on someone, there must exist a legal interest, such as a relationship by blood or marriage. For a policy in that amount, the issuing company would likely have required a medical examination and medical records.

"He was the father of her child," Braun said. "She was marrying him. Why not disclose who the insuree was? Why was she hiding it?"

The investigators also learned that Bonny had taken out a previous life insurance policy on a man they

believed might be one of many ex-husbands. There
was also information that indicated she might have
impersonated a doctor in order to certify that the in-
sured person was healthy. The detectives discovered
credit cards, airline frequent-flyer cards, a Tennessee
bank account, and other identification bearing the
name of a Dr. Christina Carol Scheier among Bonny's
papers.

Further investigation showed that Scheier was one
of Bonny's many aliases, which they tied to the Studio City post office box that Bonny had rented in
April while living at Blake's home. However, they
learned that Scheier was not a fictitious name. Scheier
was a real person and a longtime friend of Bonny's.
Scheier told investigators that she believed that Bonny
had stolen her birth certificate at one point.

The new development prompted a new theory: Had
Bonny taken the life insurance policy on Robert Blake
without his knowing it? And if so, was it possible that
she had been planning to do away with *him* in order
to collect on it? The theory explored the possibility
or likelihood of whether Bonny had perhaps hired a
hit man to kill Blake only to have the hit man back
out of the deal and kill her instead to eliminate her as
a witness to the intended action. Although the police
looked into it, they didn't get very far—if they did,
they weren't talking.

They also explored the possibility that Blake might
have ordered a hit man to kill Bonny. After all, there
were fairly large sums of cash taken out of the bank
prior to Bonny's death—at least $15,000 on one oc-

casion, and $30,000 on another. The money was supposedly given to Bonny so that she could make a couple of trips back East to visit her relatives and friends. But it was a lot of money for domestic travel.

Braun said that large amounts of money were indeed taken out of Blake's bank account prior to Bonny's murder, but it was evidence that she was using the baby to extort money from Blake and not used by Blake to hire a hit man.

"There was a lot of cash paid to her because she was basically extorting him for the custody of the child at that point," Braun said.

The question of whether Bonny's marriage to Blake, as well as to other men, was even legal had to be looked at. There was evidence that she had married several men and had not divorced all of them.

One such marriage involved that of 84-year-old DeMart Besly of Darby, Montana. Following their marriage several years earlier, DeMart and Bonny went to Elko, Nevada for their honeymoon. DeMart told reporters that he gave Bonny a roll of quarters to play the slot machines in the hotel casino where they stayed, after which he never saw her again.

"We never even consummated the marriage," he said.

According to her sister, Margerry, Bonny was only 15 when she married a man who responded to one of her letters.

"I only knew him as 'The Greek,' " Marjerry said. "The marriage lasted less than a year, and he was violent toward her. Bonny eventually got him deported."

In all, estimates of her numerous marriages topped 100. No one, probably not even Bonny, knew the precise number of times she had been wed.

"When someone dies, usually you start thinking, 'She wasn't really a bad person,' " Paul Gawron, her first husband, said. "But the truth is, Bonny was . . . A reporter called and told me that she had been killed. I wasn't surprised. She was always a dreamer. She chased her dream, and when she finally got it, it killed her."

Gawron, despite all the problems his marriage to Bonny had caused him, remained friends with her over the years. Gawron, as well as others, portrayed Bonny as a woman who survived by her wits—at the expense of naive and unsuspecting men—during her obsessive search for a celebrity that she could marry.

"She had an affair with Christian Brando, too, and was playing him and Blake off each other," Gawron said. "She would call and ask me, 'Which guy should I go with? Robert can be awfully mean.' I told her, 'Christian Brando has already killed someone. You ought to go with Robert Blake. It seems safer to me.' I'll always feel guilty for giving her that advice. I believe it killed her . . . Bonny lived a life of lies. She cheated constantly while we were married. Bonny was starstruck. She always believed that she would make it big in show business. She finally gave it up and told me, 'If I can't be a star, then I'll marry a star.' "

Gawron told reporters that he helped raise three of

Bonny's children: Glenn, 21; Holly, 20; and Jeri Lee, 7.

"I don't know for sure if any of these kids are biologically mine," Gawron said.

She eventually told him that she had obtained a Mexican divorce. Gawron said that he was aware of Bonny's marriage to Robert Moon, a truck driver, which lasted from 1985 to 1987, and to a man named John Ray from 1996 to 1998. Other marriages uncovered during the investigation showed that Bonny had also wed a man named William Webber in Florida in 1993, and later married Glynn H. Wolfe, the world's most married man. She was Wolfe's twenty-sixth wife.

Gawron described Bonny's business, and said that she had actually started selling nude photographs of herself when she was 17.

"There were times," Gawron said, "that she would have her porno spread out all over the table, with the kids walking through the room. She didn't care if they saw the pictures or not. I hated it, but I was just a laborer. When I worked I could make maybe $150 a week, and she was pulling that much and more out of envelopes every single day."

In addition to selling nude photos of herself, Bonny also operated a phone-sex line for a time.

All the while, Bonny made the rounds in Las Vegas and Los Angeles in her search for a star to wed. Among those she claimed to have had a relationship with were Redd Foxx, Chubby Checker, and Frankie

Valli, though Valli vehemently denied even knowing her.

"And when she started dating Christian Brando and met Robert Blake, she thought she'd hit the big time," Gawron said.

According to her daughter, Holly Gawron, Bonny was determined to trap Blake by getting herself pregnant by him. While telling Blake that she was taking birth-control pills, she was actually taking fertility drugs. Apparently Bonny even wrote Blake a letter and told him that she had become pregnant the first time that they ever had sex which, according to the letter, had been at a Holiday Inn on September 3, 1999.

Blake apparently had attempted to persuade Bonny to get an abortion upon learning of her pregnancy, but she wouldn't agree to it. It wasn't, however, until six months after Rose was born that she and Blake were wed, a marriage in which Bonny paid for their wedding bands. According to Paul Gawron's mother, Doris Berry, Bonny even had to pay for her hotel room on their honeymoon.

Shortly before her death, according to letters Bonny had written, she was planning to file a lawsuit against Blake over the custody agreement they had signed regarding Rose, which she did not believe was legal. The custody agreement, in part, stated that Bonny's family could not visit her at Blake's property without his express written consent, even though they were married.

"My mother may have signed her death warrant

with her plans for a suit against Blake," Holly Gawron, said. "She told me, 'If he doesn't want to have
anything to do with me, I may as well get some
money out of this.' . . . In a strange way, she finally
got her wish. She's famous now."

CHAPTER 13

BONNY LEE BAKLEY MAY HAVE BEEN AFFLICTED with a relatively new condition known as *celebriphilia* for most of her teenage and adult life. The condition itself is actually older than the term that describes it. The term celebriphilia was recently brought to light in the June 22, 2001 edition of *Entertainment Weekly* in an article about the Bakley case entitled, "Dangerous Game," by Benjamin Svetkey with Allison Hope Weiner. It is intended to describe a distinct condition as opposed to those affecting groupies and star stalkers. An afflicted celebriphiliac is indeed quite different.

A celebriphiliac, as exemplified by Bonny Lee Bakley, is attracted to famous men as opposed to merely being an overzealous fan looking for fast and unattached sex with a celebrity. Bonny Bakley had a compulsive attraction to men of celebrity and to fame itself—it was what she lived for and it became a goal she was compelled to attain.

"People who follow stars often have the obsessive-compulsive trait," said Donald Fleming, a Los Angeles psychotherapist. "They can fool almost anybody. They become so acute at reading how to meet another person's needs that they can pick up on their vulnerabilities and play them like a violin.

"Often these people have serious identity problems," Fleming continued. "They lack a centered sense of self. They're usually people that have not developed out of their grandiose childhood wishes and fantasies to be important. The only way they can feel important or special or unique is through famous people being part of their life."

"The operative word here is resourcefulness," said Dr. Michael Zona, profiler of such people for Omega Threat Management Group, a Los Angeles-based security agency that provides services to celebrities. "These folks are extremely resourceful and clever."

Bonny Bakley's resourcefulness was apparent in her address book, which Harland Braun recently made public with the addresses, and sometimes telephone numbers, blacked out.

"Let me show you something," Braun said as he flipped through its pages for reporters. "It's really disgusting . . . This lady was completely wacko. She was absolutely evil."

The book contained 17 entries, including addresses for Robert Redford, Sylvester Stallone, Gary Busey, Sugar Ray Leonard, comedian Chuck McCann, Robert De Niro, Prince, Jimmy Swaggart (a disgraced televangelist and cousin of Jerry Lee Lewis), *Hustler* publisher Larry Flynt, actor James Best, Pat McCormick, Will Jordan, Chuck Berry, Lou Christie, Frankie Valli, Dean Martin and, of course, Robert Blake. There were other listings besides the aforementioned celebrities—men of prominence and wealth, like a cattle rancher in Oklahoma and a man in San Francisco who owned racehorses and played the stock market.

Braun also made public copies of her "day log," typewritten notes detailing the progress, or lack thereof, of the famous and/or wealthy men she had set out to pursue. An example: "Send # to Gary Busey; Tulsa, OK, mother is Virginia, will forward mail." There was also a "young and rich" section as well as an "old and rich" section. In one entry under the "young and rich" segment Bonny included a reminder to send Sugar Ray Leonard, a former middleweight boxing champion, her telephone number. She also included documentation that she had left a message for a man in San Francisco—"makes $170,000 a year, owns racehorses, and plays the stock market." In an entry in the "old and rich" section she reminded herself to send a letter to the cattle rancher in Oklahoma—"owns a 320-acre cattle ranch, if he finds a girl that is true, faithful and committed to him at his death she would be financial [sic] secure," and signed it "Sylvia," one of many aliases she had used.

Bonny's resourcefulness, not to mention her persistence, as a celebriphiliac was also evident in the aggressive manner in which she pursued a relationship with Jerry Lee Lewis for years.

"She was all over us," recalled J. W. Whitten, Lewis's former road manager. "She would always stay in the same hotels we were in. She popped up at one of his birthday parties. Once she offered me money to tell her where he was. She actually thought she had a shot at being Jerry's girlfriend."

The problem of celebriphiliacs like Bonny Bakley

was prevalent enough, especially in Hollywood, that the police there have received special training to learn how to recognize it and deal with it.

"Celebrities don't like to talk about it," said Thor Merich, a detective with the Burbank police department's Criminal Intelligence Division. "Stars are sensitive about it getting out, so a lot of times we bury it. But this happens a lot. The only thing that makes Bakley's case unusual is that she was successful. She married the guy."

"In many respects," attorney Cary Goldstein said, "she was no different than the vast majority of American men and women who, given the choice, would love to marry a celebrity. She was just more aggressive about it."

"I hate the word *has-been*," continued Merich, "but common sense tells you that the B-list people have more of a problem [with celebriphiliacs]. They don't have handlers and can't afford top-notch security. And they tend to visit the same places over and over again, because people know them there and they still get the attention they crave. They leave themselves open to this problem . . . you have to get into the psyche of the celebrity. Because as much as they complain about it, these people like being famous. They like walking down the street and having people say, 'Oh my gosh, that's so-and-so.' That's why they became a celebrity in the first place. And your B-list people aren't getting that attention anymore. So they're much more susceptible to groupies or hangers-on or somebody like this Bakley woman."

"I've been in this business for ten years, and these

sorts of cases have been a constant," said John C. Lane Jr., formerly the lead officer in an LAPD celebrity protection unit and now employed by Omega Threat Management Group. "There has always been an undercurrent of inappropriate pursuit in the entertainment industry. Usually it gets dealt with behind the scenes."

The investigation continued with still few words from the LAPD on their progress, or lack thereof. Many kept returning to the days right after Nicole Brown Simpson and Ron Goldman were slain. Those were considered by many to be the most notorious murders ever committed in the history of the entertainment community. Comparisons were made between the O. J. case and the Blake case, again and again. Taken on the surface, some of the similarities were a bit uncanny.

For instance, a celebrity's wife was murdered by an apparent phantom who appeared out of nowhere. As in the O. J. case there was a guest house behind Blake's home, though it was occupied by his wife and not someone like Kato Kaelin. An Italian restaurant plays a part in both cases: Nicole Simpson had dinner at Mezzaluna on the night she was murdered, and Ron Goldman worked there; Robert Blake and Bonny Bakley ate at Vitello's shortly before Bonny was murdered. And, as in the O. J. case, the slow-moving police investigation seemed focused on the celebrity as the primary suspect.

Also making the rounds was a lot of talk regarding Blake's personality by people who knew and worked with him. Some said that his explosive emotions always ran near the surface, though those talking said that they found it difficult to believe that Blake could commit murder.

"If Bob was the kind of man who kills people, he would have killed me years ago," said Roy Huggins, who served as the executive producer of *Baretta*. Huggins said that it wasn't unusual for Blake to act out physically on the set, but he was not violent. "We had a relationship that became rather heavy. At times we would throw scripts at each other."

During one discussion that became rather heated, Huggins said that Blake confronted executive assistant, Joe Swerling.

"He said something to Joe that was typical tough guy talk," Huggins said. "Joe looked at him and said, 'Oh, now the tough talk starts,' and that was the end of it."

Stephen J. Cannell, the creator of the show, said that Blake often exhibited a bad-boy image, but added that it was all part of Blake being an obsessive perfectionist.

"He's one of those guys who's not best suited to be the star of a television series," Cannell said. "He has very strong opinions about everything. If he were doing a feature film, he could read the material and decide if he wanted to play it or not. The trouble with a television series is, you've got to shoot it and get it on the air. It all made him crazy . . . He was very passionate . . . he did a lot of rewriting."

Even Blake's membership in Alcoholics Anonymous made it into the newspapers after his wife's murder.

"Even back in the '60s, when we were all indulging," said one of Blake's longtime friends, "he was in my opinion the least of the indulgers . . . he likes his image to be the tough guy, the guy who's ready to explode. He says things like, 'I was freakin' out,' or 'I was getting the baseball bat out,' that sort of thing. But he made himself into that guy. He's really laid back, very articulate, very funny. He's his own invention, really. He's an actor."

Carl Hose, a longtime fan of Blake's and who runs an Internet website devoted to *Baretta*, told *The Philadelphia Daily News*, "I want to believe him. But there are some weird things—if he thought she was being stalked, why did he walk a block and a half away and leave her in the car, with the window open? It sounds too much like a Baretta episode [the first episode] . . . where he was going to get married and they were coming out of the restaurant and the Mafia killed her . . . my fiancée automatically thinks that he did it."

Others on the Internet, on Yahoo! message boards, kept cyberspace abuzz for weeks with talk of the murder and the fact that Blake was being considered a suspect. "Robert Blake has always been a favorite of mine, but this sounds very suspicious," wrote one poster. "I hope that I'm wrong and he is cleared of any wrongdoing."

There was even a report of one of Blake's early therapy sessions that made the news in which he lost control when the nightmarish memories of his childhood came rushing back. Blake thought that he had killed his therapist after he had grabbed him by his tie.

"I saw his glasses tilted, his face getting red and swelling up," Blake said in an interview he'd done years ago with one of the tabloid magazines. "He started coughing. Frothy bubbles were leaking from his mouth and his eyes were bulging. The next thing I knew I was in my car." But he had no memory of how he had gotten there from the therapist's office. "It hit me—'I killed him. I'm a murderer.' I sat there thinking, 'My life is over. I'll be in prison and my kids will never see me again.' I was still sitting there frozen two hours later when the therapist walked out of the building and I realized I didn't actually kill him. To this day I don't remember everything that happened in that office. And when I hear someone say, 'Well, I killed six people but I don't remember it,' I think maybe they really don't."

Blake, who a number of times over the years expressed his fascination with murder and murderers, revealed in that same interview how much he was drawn into the role of murderer Perry Smith in *In Cold Blood*.

"It was the greatest experience of my life," Blake said. "I felt like a killer. And I liked it. It was an exciting feeling of having found myself. It was buried inside me and suddenly surfaced."

CHAPTER 14

SOME EIGHT MONTHS BEFORE BONNY LEE BAKLEY was murdered, according to Bakley family attorney Cary Goldstein and Robert Blake's former assistant, Cody Blackwell, 59, Blake allegedly conned Blackwell into helping him carry out an unusual plot to kidnap his own baby. According to Blackwell, a mother of two who are now grown, Blake duped her into posing as his live-in nanny as part of a plan to get Bonny to turn over the infant without realizing what was going on. He also purportedly hired two men to pose as police officers to frighten Bonny into going back to Arkansas without the child. The plan even called for a camouflage-wearing bodyguard to "take care" of Bonny if the plan went awry.

Evidence would show that Blake had previously tried to persuade Bonny to have an abortion, she recorded the phone conversations and they would eventually make their way first into the hands of editors at a tabloid magazine and later into the hands of the LAPD. However, after seeing baby Rose after she was born, Blake had a change of heart about not wanting the child and became obsessed with getting custody.

According to the reports, Blake hatched the plan in September 2000, while Bonny was serving the terms of her probation in Arkansas, arranging to have Bonny bring Rose, then three months old, out to California for a visit under the guise that they would discuss their marriage plans. Prior to Bonny and the baby's arrival, Blake called Blackwell, who had worked for him in the past, and asked her to move into his home to care for the infant girl.

"He didn't tell me very much," Blackwell said. "All he said was how awful the child's mother was. He said she was involved with the Russian Mafia, biker groups, and drug dealing. He said, 'She thinks she is coming here to get married. But I can tell you she has another thought coming.' Then he said, 'I will do anything to get my hands on that child.' I was shocked by what I was hearing."

The day that Bonny was scheduled to arrive, Blackwell told investigators, Blake introduced her to a man that he identified only as "Moose." Moose was a big guy, approximately six feet tall and weighing about 250 pounds, and he had shoulder-length hair.

"I realized then that something was wrong, but I still didn't know what was going to happen," Blackwell said. When Blake showed up at the house with Bonny and the baby, Moose hid from view inside a utility room.

"Robert introduced me to Bonny as his nanny, 'Nancy.' He told Bonny I would help her with the baby, and she handed her to me. Then he said he and Bonny were going for lunch and left the baby with me. Bonny said that she had to change the little girl's diaper, but he told her not to worry, that I was a fully trained nanny and I could do all of that."

Blackwell said that Blake called her on the telephone about ten minutes later and instructed her to immediately leave his house and to take the baby with her to her apartment. Blackwell, who lived in a Hollywood Hills apartment with her two large dogs, an Alaskan malamute and a dog that was part wolf, flew into a panic.

"I had no idea that I was involved in the kidnapping of a child until we were halfway through," Blackwell said.

When Blackwell arrived at her apartment, she laid the baby on the bed and the part-wolf dog jumped onto the bed next to her. Rose was contented, and seemed to enjoy playing with the dog's soft hair. As Blackwell calmed down and composed herself from all the excitement she had just been put through, she suddenly realized what had occurred.

"My head was spinning," Blackwell said. "I couldn't believe that I was getting involved in a child kidnapping."

The investigators were not immediately able to determine which restaurant Bonny and Blake had gone to for lunch that day, but they reasoned that it must have been close by. After all, he had called Blackwell with instructions to take the baby and leave within ten minutes, but he would have had to separate himself from Bonny for a short time in order to make the call without her hearing it. The investigators reasoned that he would likely have had to be inside the restaurant in order to accomplish that, leaving them wondering if he had taken her to Vitello's that day, only five minutes away from his house.

Although they were unable to immediately determine where Blake and Bonny had gone that day, a relatively minor detail, the investigators were able to corroborate Blackwell's account of what happened by talking with Bakley's sister, Margerry.

"Before Bonny died," Margerry said, "she told me he had persuaded her to leave the baby with the nanny in the house while they went for a meal. Once in the restaurant, two cops came in and told her she was there illegally and that she had to go back to Arkansas because she was on probation."

Blake, according to what Bonny had purportedly told her sister, had pretended to appear worried, and advised Bonny that she should go with them and assured her that he would have the baby brought to her later on.

"In the car," Margerry said, "one of the cops told her he was only a week away from retirement and didn't want to get involved with all of the paperwork, so if she just flew back home and reported to her probation officer, he wouldn't take any more action. It was only when she got back to Little Rock that she found out these two people weren't real police officers at all."

After Blake had Rose in his possession, according to Margerry, Bonny seldom saw the child. Blake apparently kept the infant at his daughter's home in Hidden Hills, away from Bonny. Bonny had initiated court action through her attorney, Cary Goldstein, but backed off after Blake asked her to marry him.

According to Goldstein, Bonny had only been allowed to see the baby when guards were present.

"It was a kidnapping," Goldstein said. "She was going to court claiming kidnapping . . . then she asked

me to call it off because she wanted to get along with
Blake. This was before paternity was proven."

According to Blackwell's account of how Blake retrieved the baby from her, Blake had called her approximately 45 minutes after she had arrived home
that day with the baby and had instructed her to meet
him on a street corner in Studio City. He was alone.

"Robert picked up the baby and I heard him say,
'Well, kid, it's just you and me from now on,'"
Blackwell said. However, Rose began to cry and
Blake was unable to get her to stop. "He turned to me
and said, 'Okay, you're going to have to come with
me.'"

Blackwell said that Blake then instructed her to get
into the back of his sport utility vehicle, the one with
the personalized license plate that reads, "SAYZ-
WHO," and to lie down with the baby.

"I don't think he wanted me to know where we
were going," Blackwell said. "But I recognized the
route to Calabasas [and Hidden Hills]. I knew his
daughter, Delinah, lived there."

Before arriving at his destination, Blackwell said
that Blake dropped her off at a McDonald's and gave
her money to buy something to eat, and then drove
off. He was gone for about an hour, and when he
returned the baby was not with him. She said she also
saw a side of Blake that she didn't like, one that dis-
turbed her greatly.

"I knew he must have left her with Delinah," she
said. "All the way back he was ranting and raving.
He told me, 'Just let them come for me. Just let them
try, I've got guns. I'll pick them off one by one as

they come over my fence. I'll leave their bones in the yard for the birds.' " She said that she told him that what he had done was wrong.

"He told me," she said, " 'The trouble with you, Cody, is that you live your life like Mary Poppins. Nice guys always finish last.' "

When they arrived back at his home in Studio City, Blackwell said that Blake gave her $300, which was her normal rate of pay for one week's work. She said that she called him later, after arriving home, and told him that she wasn't happy about being involved in his kidnapping plot, and that she never spoke to him again.

"But I called him on the day before Bonny was killed, just to see how he was," Blackwell said. "I left a message on his answering machine, but I didn't hear back from him. A couple of days later I heard about the shooting of his wife. I was just shocked. I just couldn't believe that he had married this woman. I am convinced that the baby's kidnapping started a chain of events that led to murder."

Margerry Bakley, meanwhile, went on nationally televised talk shows and spoke to tabloid newspapers to express her opinion that it was obvious that Robert Blake had killed her sister.

"We'd known about it for over a year that he's been plotting this," Margerry said. "Unfortunately, I couldn't stop her with her obsessional love for him." She said that her family knew that he was plotting Bonny's death just from the things Bonny talked about when she called and wrote about in letters to Margerry and her mother. "He tried to hire my brother, to do a hit last year. It was insane."

"Bonny told me about how he threatened her," Margerry said. "He said he had a bullet with her name on it. He told her he wanted the baby, but didn't want Bonny. She knew she was in danger, but she just wanted to be with him. He offered her money to pay her off, but she wouldn't take it. I told her time and time again to get out, but she wouldn't. She tried all her life to get married to a famous person, and now she'd finally done it. It didn't matter how bad the marriage was."

Although Margerry said that she had never met Blake, contending that she had refused to meet him because she didn't like the things she had been hearing about him, she said that Bonny had conveyed to her that Blake was scary.

"Sometimes he was kind," Margerry said her sister had told her. "Not generous, and just a frightening man, but she was obsessed in love with him."

Margerry characterized her sister as unstable, and said that it was her instability that had played a part in her decision to marry someone she said she feared and who treated her badly.

According to Margery Bakley, Bonny had foreseen what was coming, namely that she would be killed at some point, and had instructed her sister to contact a person at the tabloid magazine, *The Star*. The contact person's name that Bonny had left with Margerry was Chris Bell, and Bonny had also provided Bell's phone number.

"She said, 'When it happens, call Chris Bell, and he'll do a good story on me,' " Margerry claimed her sister told her. "He's always been fair to her in the past." Margerry said that Bonny had also instructed her to "please put a good picture in," amazingly referring to a photo in which she would look her best in the magazine that would be published after her death. Even when she perceived what was going to happen to her, Bonny's concern was how she would look in the magazine. Her *celebriphilia* would live on after her death.

Margerry contended that in the early days of the investigation, detectives from the LAPD told her that the tabloid magazines were ahead of them in the investigation and that they were working to try and catch up with them. She also stated that in her discussions with the detectives, they left her with the impression that they felt that Blake was behind Bonny's death.

"I feel that they strongly believe that he's involved," Margerry said. "And they're just doing their job slowly and keeping things to themselves. And they're going to try and nail him." She said that she was praying that they do.

As the investigation into Bonny's bizarre murder continued, information surfaced that showed that Bonny had accused Blake of cheating on her and that Blake had purportedly told her on one occasion that he knew someone who would buy their baby daughter for $100,000. However, a police source downplayed the suggestion that Blake would sell his daughter.

"He genuinely loved this little girl," said the source. "In talking to him, I got the feeling it rejuvenated him and gave him a new lease on life . . . I think he only married her because he was an old-fashioned guy who wanted to do things right."

Bonny's accusations toward Blake, among other things, were revealed in excerpts from letters, undated but believed to have been written by Bonny beginning in early autumn 1999 and continuing until they signed the custody agreement regarding Rose in October 2000. An excerpt from one of the letters reads:

> "Hi. You wanted something in writing. Here it is. I, Bonny Lee Bakley, aka Lee Bonny Bakley, promise to never do any of those things the . . . lawyers . . . told Michael Gubitosi, aka Robert Blake, I intended to do. Unless of course, he, Michael Gubitosi, aka Robert Blake, intends to be unfaithful in this lifetime. Then who knows what I might be capable of . . . Oh, and no sex after we were married, that's another thing . . ."
>
> Bonny Lee Bakley; Lee Bonny Bakley.

Another excerpt:

> I agree of my own free will to stay out of the State of California for the next four months so that my daughter will have an opportunity to get to know her father.

Another letter, written shortly after Rose was born: "You talked to *The Enquirer*, letting them write that story to try to embarrass me, my friends, and family . . . Oh yeah, the $100,000-offer for the baby, telling me someone you know wanted to buy her. I knew it was you just trying to get rid of me, thinking that would be cheaper than paying child support in the long run. All of this is enough to make any sane person temporarily insane . . . Anyway, if there is any way at all possible to get past all this I still want to be with you forever, with no lies or cheating, of course. If you really don't want this . . . then let me know." It was signed: "Lee Bonny."

In another letter, Bonny accused Blake of having an affair with a woman in New York while she was giving birth to Rose. It was then that she told him that the baby's father was Christian Brando, an apparent attempt to get even with him over the affair she believed he'd had. In one letter she wrote to Blake she stated, "I realize the only thing I'm getting out of this deal is a nasty old wop. But that's all I wanted. So like you tell me, relax." In yet another letter, she asked Blake to keep her visits between Arkansas and California a secret "so they don't throw me back in jail."

In another of her letters, believed to have been written in September 2000 while she was still in Arkansas, Bonny expressed a sense of fear that she might be in danger if she returned to California.

"I'm almost afraid to move out," she wrote. "Perhaps someone will set me up or something." It wasn't clear who she was referring to, but it was possible that she had made the comment in reference to someone out of her past, one of the many men that she had bilked out of varying amounts of money over her 20-year career as a con woman.

The letters, of course, were all one-sided and all

Bonny, and they provided no clues as to whether Blake was ever in love with her or not.

As the detectives continued looking into the claims about the mysterious man that had been seen lurking about outside Blake's home prior to Bonny's murder, information surfaced that indicated Bonny had attempted to reignite her romance with Christian Brando less than a month before she was murdered. According to the reports, Brando told a friend that he had received a love letter from Bonny and that it had been followed up by a telephone call from her. The information was made public to refute what a friend of Bonny's said during a television interview, namely that Brando had been actively seeing Bonny in the weeks before she died.

"Bakley sent along pictures of her child when she wrote to Christian in April saying she wanted to reconcile with him," according to a friend of Christian's who revealed the information. "A few days later, Christian said he received a telephone call from Bonny. The call scared him. He said to me, 'I told her it was best for her to leave me alone.' "

Apparently, following Bonny's murder, Christian's father, Marlon Brando, fearful that Christian might be unduly dragged into the murder investigation because of his criminal record, instructed his son to get in touch with his former attorney, Robert Shapiro.

"Christian told Shapiro he hadn't seen Bonny, but had received a letter and call from her," said Brando's friend. "Christian doesn't want to be involved in any more police matters."

When the information came to light, Christian's

mother, Anna Kashfi, told reporters that her son had already suffered enough from his previous problems.

"I've no doubt the killing has brought back awful memories of that night of May 16, 1990," Kashfi said, "when Christian killed his sister's boyfriend, Dag Drolett, in a fit of anger that he'll regret all his life. Christian hadn't seen Bonny for eighteen months, and their romance was over. Robert Blake saw to that when he stole Bonny from Christian, which, as far as I'm concerned, was a lucky break for my son."

Nonetheless, LAPD investigators were preparing to question Christian Brando about Bonny's life, her relationship with him, and ultimately her death.

CHAPTER 15

As the investigators from the LAPD's Robbery-Homicide Division were making plans to interview Christian Brando about his connections to Bonny Lee Bakley, friends of Bonny's came forward and told reporters that Bonny had indeed reignited her affair with Christian and was with him only weeks before she was murdered. According to Bonny's friends, she was madly in love with Brando and had been thrilled when she became pregnant because she had thought that he was the father. That's why she initially named the girl Christian Shannon Brando. However, when DNA tests later showed that the baby was Blake's, Bonny was reportedly very disappointed. One of her friends had warned her that she "was playing with fire" by trying to rekindle her relationship with Brando, but Bonny apparently wouldn't listen to the advice that was being offered to her.

One friend, Tina Miller, told a reporter that Bonny had called her about three weeks before she was murdered to tell her that she was with Christian.

"It was around midnight on the West Coast," Miller said, "and she said she was at Christian's house and he was in bed. She even called me back and said she was torn between Blake and Brando."

Miller said that she had warned Bonny that she was playing a dangerous game, to no avail.

" 'You're going back and forth, and you're married now,' " Miller said she told her. But Bonny wouldn't listen to her friend. "She always thought she could do what she wanted to do."

Another friend, Ray Hale, told a reporter that Bonny was obsessed with Brando.

"She was madly in love with him," Hale said. "He's the only man she truly ever loved. When she found out the baby was Blake's, she was deeply disappointed. She kept hoping the baby was Christian's because she desperately wanted to marry him."

Brando, through his attorney, Robert Shapiro—who assisted in O. J. Simpson's defense—denied that he had seen Bonny and said that he hadn't talked to her for at least 18 months.

"He is not involved in any way whatsoever," declared Shapiro. "He's tried his best to stay out of the media and live a quiet and private life."

Amid all of the talk and speculation being circulated about Bonny having reunited with Christian Brando while married to Robert Blake, the LAPD began investigating a purported secret meeting that was said to have occurred only a few days before Bonny was murdered. The LAPD's inquiry was supposedly initiated to establish whether or not Bakley's murder could have involved a conspiracy. Although the LAPD investigators weren't talking about that leg of their investigation, or any other for that matter, a friend of Bonny's, Judy Howell, revealed to reporters details of Bonny's fears that a meeting between Marlon Brando and Robert Blake was going to occur.

"Bonny called me two weeks before she was shot,"

Howell said, "and said she was scared because Blake had told her that he was going to see Marlon Brando. When Bonny asked him why, he just chuckled and told her, 'When you find out, it'll be too late.' " According to what Howell said Bonny had told her, Blake also told her that "Marlon has a lot of Mafia connections."

When reporters got hold of the information, they naturally tried to contact Marlon Brando for comment. However, when they reached his agent, he refused to talk about it. One of Brando's longtime friends, however, told the newshounds that it was ridiculous to think that Marlon Brando and Robert Blake would plot someone's murder together. Brando's friend also stated that he did not have any Mafia connections. Furthermore, said the friend, Blake and Brando were merely old friends who enjoyed each other's company.

However, record producer Robert Stefanow, Bonny's longtime friend and alleged former lover, told reporters an account that indicated Bonny's fear of such a meeting. Stefanow also said that both Blake and Brando had more than sufficient reason to hate Bonny.

"Bonny was terrified that Robert's meeting with Marlon would lead to her death," Stefanow said. "She even asked me and another friend, 'Do you think Robert is asking Marlon's help to plan a hit on me?' . . . Blake hated her because she wouldn't give him custody of their child and because she had tricked him into getting her pregnant by pretending to use birth control. And Brando didn't like her because she had tried to entrap his son Christian into marriage."

Stefanow told reporters that he had been questioned by LAPD detectives for several hours, and the Blake/Brando meeting had come up during their interview.

"Two detectives flew from Los Angeles to my home in New Jersey to interview me on May 15," Stefanow said. "They told me that they have eight full-time detectives assigned to this case and were very interested in what I had to say . . . Blake's private meeting with Marlon Brando was one of the topics I discussed with the cops."

According to Judy Howell, Bonny's fear of the meeting between Blake and Brando stemmed in part from the fact that she knew that Marlon was aware of a plan she had to entrap Christian so that she could get a piece of his fortune. This plan was confirmed in letters obtained by the police that Bonny had sent to family members, and friends, in which she had written that she hoped that the baby was Christian's because it would give her access to his famous dad's money. LAPD detectives met with Howell at her home in Mississippi on May 17, where they questioned her for about four hours.

"The police told me they confirmed a meeting between Blake and Marlon had taken place and they were interested in what I knew about it," Howell told reporters. "They are clearly trying to find out if the two of them were plotting against Bonny."

Despite what was being stated in the press about a meeting between Marlon Brando and Robert Blake, the LAPD remained tight-lipped and would neither confirm or deny the reports that were making the news.

* * *

Even though Bonny's autopsy report remained sealed from the public, people close to the investigation revealed that her autopsy indicated that she likely knew and trusted the person who killed her.

"Bonny's wounds and the absence of any defensive marks suggest that she was shot before she had a chance to show fear or react," the source told news reporters. "Investigators have concluded that she was quite comfortable being close to whomever did it. If women are scared of someone approaching, they typically lift their hands to shield their face. In tragic cases where they are shot during robberies, they often raise both hands and there are what are termed 'shots through' wounds on the hands."

According to the source, the autopsy results show that Bonny was shot once in the shoulder and once in the head at nearly point-blank range. Although the shoulder wound would have been potentially fatal, it had been the shot to the head that killed her.

The unnamed source who spoke with reporters said that the crime scene investigators had at first thought a robbery might have been involved and, as such, had expected to find broken or shattered glass at the scene of the crime.

"They thought Bonny Lee might have been shot through the window when she slammed the door on an attacker," said the source. "But they quickly saw a different picture," when they found that none of the windows had been shattered. The informant also said that the pathologists performed toxicology tests to determine if the presence of drugs or alcohol were in Bonny's system.

"There was also a test done to see if she had recent sexual intercourse," the informant said. "But it was inconclusive."

Meanwhile, famed and respected Allegheny County, Pennsylvania coroner and forensic pathologist Cyril Wecht, who is also an attorney, jumped into the three-ring circus of media madness that continued to revolve around Bonny Lee Bakley's murder and offered his two cents' worth of theory and conjecture. According to Wecht, two shots fired could be an indication that the killer was not a professional hit man.

"Two shots could indicate that the killer was not a trained assassin, who would be steely enough to only need one shot through the head," Wecht told reporters. "One could argue that the lack of broken glass in the street might show she knew and trusted her killer because she didn't roll up the window."

The autopsy report, when it is eventually released, will show a great deal of detail, according to Wecht.

"Any fractures or bruises on her body will be mentioned, as well as previous surgery scars," Wecht said. "The internal exam will track the trajectory of the bullet. A bullet enters the body making a small circular hole, and then blasts out with a larger, irregularly shaped hole. Therefore, if the bullet entered her facial area, it might travel through her brain and exit from the back or side of the head, spraying blood, bone, and brain matter on the headrest or car interior."

During the initial reports right after the shooting,

details such as those outlined by Wecht were not mentioned. Tests, however, were being conducted to determine the distance between the perpetrator and Bakley when the gun was fired.

"Gunpowder stipling might have been left on her flesh or clothing," Wecht said, "indicating that the shooter was closer than two feet away when the shots were fired."

It should be noted that blood spatter from a gunshot often produces a very high percentage of fine specks of blood, a mistlike dispersion that is similar to an aerosol spray. The blood spatter's low mass seldom travels a horizontal distance of more than three to four feet. There is also the issue of blood back spatter, which usually occurs less than three inches from the muzzle to the target area when blood is found inside the gun's barrel. It is also important to note that the bullet's caliber determines how far blood back spatter makes it into the gun's barrel. Normally, the larger the bullet's caliber is the greater the depth into the gun's barrel blood can be found. There is normally less back spatter in terms of concentration and penetration in recoil auto-loading guns than in guns whose barrels do not recoil.

Since the LAPD isn't talking, it isn't publicly known, yet, whether blood was found inside the barrel of the Walther PPK that was used to murder Bonny. Since the Walther PPK fires a medium-caliber bullet, it can reasonably be expected that blood spatter would be present in the gun's barrel—how much, of course, is dependent upon how close the shooter had been to Bonny when the gun was fired.

According to Wecht, the determination of whether Bonny had first been shot in the head and then the shoulder, or vice versa, could have a major impact upon the prosecution of the perpetrator if this case made it to trial.

"If the shoulder wound came first," Wecht said, "there might have been a period of a few seconds during which the victim knew she was doomed and begged for her life or tried to escape. That fear factor could be considered extra pain and suffering, upping the penalty that prosecutors could demand."

Meanwhile, former LAPD detective-turned-author Mark Fuhrman came forward with his assessment of the case and the investigation by stating that he thinks the Bonny Bakley murder case is a replica of the O. J. Simpson case, which he worked on. Fuhrman, 49, chimed in with Bakley's relatives by stating in *The Globe* tabloid newspaper that he believes Robert Blake will eventually be charged with his wife's murder.

"According to the family of Blake's wife, Bonny Lee Bakley, there is evidence of domestic violence, and someone has made threats on her life," Fuhrman said. "What I see is an out-of-control relationship here, and that's what domestic violence murder is. As a society, we can't believe that celebrities are capable of murder. But that doesn't mean they aren't. Because O. J. was someone who made us laugh, we couldn't accept that he could kill Nicole Brown and Ronald Goldman. Blake wasn't as popular as O. J., still he's not a guy we see as a killer. But everyone is capable of murder, including O. J. and Blake."

Fuhrman stated that his former colleagues at the LAPD probably considered Blake guilty.

"He's definitely a suspect," Fuhrman said. "The LAPD is not treating Blake as a grieving husband, and he's not acting like one. A grieving husband doesn't run out the moment his wife is murdered and get an attorney he's never hired before. That's what we [cops] call 'lawyering up,' and grieving husbands don't do that. My take is he's the only suspect."

During Fuhrman's interview with *The Globe*, he took the opportunity to pick apart Blake's story and point out the holes in it.

"He was so afraid that he had to carry a gun," Fuhrman said. "But then he forgets it in a restaurant and leaves his wife alone? How do you lose your gun on the very night your wife gets shot in the head and murdered? How could you leave your wife alone like that if she was afraid for her life and being stalked? And who was this stalker? No one's seen him. He doesn't have a description or name. Why would you leave her alone like that when you can drive back to the restaurant? And it's LA, so why not use valet parking? Even if we buy the scorned-lover motive, the most Bonny Lee ever got out of an ex-lover was $2,500. This murder was an act of rage. Blake's story just doesn't add up."

"He's got a cloud over him," Harland Braun reiterated in a reference to his client. "But you have to live with who you are, make your peace with your maker about who you really are and not what people perceive you as. He's learning that lesson very quickly . . . The

LAPD is investigating Mr. Blake and his involvement in this case thoroughly. So whether you call him a suspect or a subject or a witness doesn't really matter."

On Wednesday, May 16, the subject of whether or not Bonny Bakley was a victim of her own plot against Blake came up again, primarily because of what Blake's bodyguard, Earle Caldwell, told the police, namely that he believed that Bonny had tried to arrange for someone to kill Blake.

"If Blake was killed, she would get $13,000 a month in child support," Braun said. "Caldwell's theory is that she hired someone to kill Blake and the guys thought she was so unstable that they killed her instead and kept the money." However, Braun admitted that the evidence to support such a theory was not very strong.

Bakley family attorney Cary Goldstein called Blake's version of what happened absurd. "I don't know whether he did it or not," Goldstein said, "but his story is absurd. Here's a man so worried about the safety of his wife that he carries a gun, but then he leaves her next to a dark construction site at night, a block and a half from the restaurant in a bad neighborhood . . . This is theater of the absurd and what frightens me is that they [Blake's attorneys] are starting to sell it. Did he murder Bonny? I don't know, but certainly he's a very likely suspect."

"My dad is innocent, period," Blake's son, Noah, said, adding that there was not a shred of evidence to prove that he killed Bonny. He also pointed the finger at the media for spreading rumors that his dad was the prime suspect. "Everybody is pointing to him and trying to create a story here . . . He does not need to prove that [he's innocent] and he's not obligated nor is he obligated, to address a thousand, trillion rumors."

Braun agreed.

"If the police had any physical evidence against my client," Braun said, "they would have arrested him by now. My client is innocent . . . there's almost an infinite number of people out there with the motive to kill her."

Meanwhile, LAPD officials were again critical of Harland Braun, as well as the news media, for interfering with their investigation into Bonny's murder. Garrett Zimmon, commanding officer of LAPD's Detective Services, said that Braun's constant dialogue with the media, as well as leaks from inside the department, were beginning to interfere with the detectives' efforts to solve the murder.

In the meantime, Robert Blake dropped out of sight. It was believed that he had retreated to his daughter's home in Hidden Hills, and all that Braun would say was that he was staying with friends and relatives. His precise location could not be confirmed. It was almost a certainty, however, that the LAPD detectives investigating his wife's murder knew where he was staying. It was even said by former LAPD spokesman Tony Alba that because of Blake's battles with depression, drugs, and alcohol, not to mention the fact that his own father killed himself, it was likely that he was under a "suicide watch" by the LAPD regardless of where he was staying. Alba pointed out that investigators keep a close eye on potential suspects who were close to a homicide victim.

"They want to make sure the person's mental state is okay," Alba said. "That they are not stressed out or possibly in a mental state where they might attempt suicide."

CHAPTER 16

As THE MYSTERY CONTINUED TO UNFOLD, WHAT WAS already a most bizarre story became even more so when information surfaced regarding allegations that Robert Blake had attempted to hire Bonny Lee Bakley's brother, Joey Bakley, as a hit man for $10,000. Joey, a young construction worker who resides just across the border from San Diego in Tijuana, Mexico, told reporters that Blake called him at his home in October, 2000 and asked him to come to Los Angeles. Joey said that Blake told him that he had a proposition, a business deal that he wanted to discuss with him.

Joey claimed that he met Blake at a doughnut shop in Los Angeles. Blake insisted that he and Joey go for a stroll in a nearby park. As they walked into the park, Joey said that Blake began asking him about his past.

"I told him I'm not perfect," Joey said. "I've had a few scrapes with the law and was busted a couple of times for drug trafficking and things, but that was a long time ago. I'm all right now. So I guess he had it in his mind that I was some kind of shady character, so he said, 'Did you ever do away with someone?' I'm no fool. I knew that he was feeling me out about killing someone. So I said, 'You mean you want me to rub someone out for you?' His response stunned me. He said, 'Yeah, I do. I'll pay you $5,000 up front and more later.' I was shocked. He told me that he and two friends had invested some money with a gay guy who lives on a yacht in Rosarito, Mexico. That's not too far from my home in Tijuana. He said the guy on the boat had ripped him off and he wanted him killed."

Joey said he was curious about Blake's motive and who it was he wanted killed, so he played along and told Blake that he would think about the offer.

"He gave me a few hundred bucks," Joey said, "and said, 'Here's my private phone number. Go home and think about it and call me later, and I'll give you the $5,000 and the pictures and information about the man.' "

Joey claimed that he spoke to Blake a number of times over the next several weeks regarding the "job" he allegedly wanted him to do, although he had no intention of killing anyone for Blake, or anyone else.

"He kept wanting to know if I'd made up my mind," Joey said. "He wired me $500 by Western Union and asked me about getting him some crystal meth [a very strong methamphetamine]. Of course, I had no intention of helping this jerk kill someone. So I took his money and put him off. Then I tried to call him sometime last November, but he wouldn't take my call. I talked to Bonny and she told me, 'Robert says he was contacted by someone from the San Diego police and so he doesn't want to have anything to do with you.' I'm not sure what he was talking about. I don't think anyone from the police contacted Blake. But I sure wish they had. My sister would be alive if they had."

According to Joey, Blake felt that he had been trapped and taken advantage of by Bonny. But not only did Bonny have to pay for their wedding bands, she had to pay for her flight out from Arkansas to California for their wedding.

"After they got married," Joey said, "they fought all the time. Bonny told me that during one of the arguments, Blake threatened to kill her. My sister laughed it off. She didn't take him seriously. But after he approached me about killing someone, I knew what type of person she was dealing with. I warned her to be careful. I knew he was capable of murder . . . I told her, 'Bonny, honey, you better watch out. Blake's gonna get you.' But she just said, 'Don't you say that.' . . . He is a very scary, very bad and very evil man."

Joey explained that after Blake asked him to kill someone he felt that the actor had been feeling him out to see if he would consider killing his own sister, though the conversation never went that far.

"I don't like dealing with the cops," he said. "They wouldn't take my word over a rich, powerful Hollywood star anyway."

When he was asked about the story that Blake and his lawyers told the police regarding Bonny being stalked, Joey indicated that he didn't believe it.

"First of all, I spoke to Bonny all the time and she told me everything," Joey said. "She never mentioned that anyone was stalking her or wanted to kill her.

She had her own guns and could take care of herself. She didn't need his protection. Then, about a week before she was murdered, my sister tells me that Blake told her, 'If anything happens to either one of us, the custody of the baby should go to my daughter, Delinah.' I knew that was strange, but Bonny thought he was just being caring. Now that she's been killed, it all makes sense. He's a bloodthirsty monster who wanted to test me out by having me kill this man in Mexico. He knew that if I was prepared to do that, I'd be willing to do anything, even kill my own sister. I am convinced that he was feeling me out to see if I was lowlife enough to murder my own flesh and blood. It was only when he figured out I wouldn't do it that he went out and found someone else. There is no doubt in my mind that Robert Blake caused my sister to be killed . . ."

There is only Joey's word that the aforementioned conversation ever took place, and if it in fact had occurred, it did not mean that Blake had necessarily been serious about hiring Joey to kill someone. If Blake had merely wanted to get Bonny out of his life like she herself believed he did, it was entirely possible that Blake had set up a scenario with Joey— knowing that he would tell his sister. He may have hoped that, if she believed that was the story, it might serve to frighten her away and out of his life. The same line of reasoning might also be applied to the stories Bonny had told a friend about Blake driving Bonny around town, looking for "just the right place." On the other hand, it was also possible that Blake had been serious about his topic of discussion with Joey as well as his search for "just the right place."

At any rate, Joey was certainly one of the people that the LAPD detectives would want to talk to about his rendezvous and experiences with Robert Blake.

Robert Blake was the kind of guy who kept a loaded gun in a kitchen drawer and a drawer full of condoms in his bedroom, according to Michelle Whitman, 54, Blake's former personal assistant who provided additional insight into his personality. He was also a moody man—gracious and kind one minute, dark and angry the next. Whitman, a resident of Studio City, described him as a man with a Jekyll and Hyde personality, who tried to keep his demons under control by visiting a therapist several times a week.

"He was in therapy for a long time," Whitman said. "I believe he's a recovering alcoholic and drug addict and was also trying to give up smoking."

Whitman said that she met Blake as she walked down Dilling Street one day in 1998 and saw him working in front of his house. She said that she struck up a conversation with him and expressed an interest in working in the movies. She asked him if he knew anyone who could help her, and after chatting for about an hour he asked her if she would be interested in working as his personal assistant. When she said that she was, he hired her and she began working at The Mata Hari Ranch, the next day.

Whitman's duties consisted mostly of helping Blake with his paperwork, shopping for him and preparing his meals. She even dyed his hair for him.

"He has lots of money, so I could never understand why he didn't get it done professionally," Whitman said. "He would sit in the kitchen with a towel draped around him. I would get the chemical mixture just the way he liked it."

Sometimes, however, Blake would terrify her with his dark, angry moods, Whitman said.

"It was very unnerving working for Robert," Whitman said. "He has a deep reservoir of anger and hate. Sometimes he was nice. But he was frequently in one of his dark, terrible moods. If I did something wrong, he would just glare at me. It made me want to take a few steps back. He's a very intimidating presence. I can see why his wife was afraid of him . . . he's not someone I would want to cross. He's like an animal. He could smell when I was afraid, and would pounce . . . it was difficult for him to break away from the habits that bedeviled him. Robert used to say that he would pour Jack Daniel's or some other liquor on his hands, rub them together and breathe in the scent. He also put an unlit cigarette in his mouth just to get the sensation of smoking."

Whitman's account of Blake's personality was good background information for the cops, but it really didn't help them much as far as making progress. The purported mood swings could be important, but most people have them to some degree. It doesn't mean that they have a propensity for murder, though mood swings can sometimes be an important factor that can push an otherwise normal person over the edge.

While Bonny Lee Bakley's body still lay on a cold steel slab, in the Los Angeles County Morgue, unclaimed as yet by her next of kin, the LAPD investigators announced that they were going to retrace the trip that Blake, Bonny, and Earle Caldwell took to the Sequoia National Park in late April. They would interview the employees at the Gateway Restaurant and Lodge where the trio stayed, and would go over their earlier interview with Earle Caldwell, possibly interviewing him again. They would also inspect the two-bedroom cottage overlooking a rough portion of the Kaweah River, an area frequented by a number of Hollywood celebrities.

Anjelica Huston has a home there, and Jennifer Aniston and Brad Pitt have been seen there frequently spending the weekend together. William Shatner at one time owned property there, and he is still occasionally seen there on weekends riding a moped.

"Most of 'em ride around on their bikes and no one notices 'em," said John Elliott, a resident as well as editor and publisher of the weekly *Kaweah Commonwealth* newspaper. "And that's what they like."

Carl Wheeler, a longtime resident, said that he saw Robert Blake when he came into a local market about three years ago. Wheeler said that he was friendly.

"I said to him, 'Hey, you look familiar,' " Wheeler

said. "He said, 'Yeah, I think we were on the same cellblock in Minnesota.' I guess he got back at me."

Others, particularly employees at the Gateway Restaurant and Lodge, recalled the threesome during their stay on the weekend of April 27–29.

"They were all real friendly," Greg Mendoza said. Mendoza, a bartender and maître d', said that he spoke with them briefly while they were having dinner at the lodge's restaurant. "Everybody in the restaurant was real shocked about what happened. We had just seen them."

Mendoza recalled when they returned on the evening after their first day's outing, after Earle Caldwell had become ill and Blake came into the bar seeking assistance.

"He came in and was real concerned," Mendoza said. "He said, 'Get a doctor. I don't care what it costs.'" Contrary to earlier reports in which the trio's guide, Gary Tomlin, said that Blake had been too tired to go along, Mendoza said that Blake accompanied Caldwell to the hospital and they both returned later that night. Most of those who had seen them that weekend described Blake as being very friendly and praised him as being "a very nice man."

"He is polite, very friendly, very sociable," said Brenda Chavez, who works as a cook at the We Three Bakery where Blake occasionally ate when visiting the area. She said that Blake told her that he had been coming to the area since he was 14 years old. She also said that she didn't believe that he killed his wife and cannot understand why he has not been eliminated as a suspect.

*   *   *

Earle Caldwell, meanwhile, reiterated his earlier opinion that he didn't believe that Blake killed Bonny. "They're [the police] already cooking his goose," Caldwell said. "He had nothing to do with it." Caldwell said that his theory, the scenario involving Bonny hiring a hit man to kill Blake only to be killed by him instead, was not received well by the police. They dismissed it as "ridiculous."

"They have their minds made up about what happened and I'm sure they think Robert did it," Caldwell said. "That's all they're looking for. I wanted to tell them about the relationship he had with Bonny. About the vacation we took. They didn't want to hear about it."

"I've been closer to these people than anyone on the planet," Caldwell continued. "She [Bonny] seemed like a nice enough woman, a little scatterbrained at times, paranoid. She would say strange things for no reason."

Strange things like, he said, when she told him that she had a brother who lived in Mexico who was a hit man. It was a comment that, he said, she never repeated again in his presence. Caldwell also said that he was aware of her mail-order lonely hearts scams, and he would often take her to the post office boxes that she maintained so that she could pick up her mail.

Caldwell said that he had left town a few days before Bonny was killed because she had suggested to Blake that he fire him so her brother could take over his job. He heard the news about the murder while he was away, visiting relatives in the San Francisco Bay area, and said that Blake had called him to assure him that he was going to be okay.

"I think they missed the person they were after," Caldwell said of the person who might have been hired to perform the hit. "I think they were after Robert . . . maybe they made a mistake. That would be my gut feeling. Why else would she want me out of the way that weekend?"

Caldwell also said that he was surprised that the police had not yet fingerprinted him and named him as a possible suspect in Bonny's death.

"If I were the police I'd be looking at me as the number-one suspect," he said.

Life had been happier at Blake's residence in the weeks before Bonny's murder, Caldwell said. Blake and Bonny had been getting along much better, and he knew that they had been having sex together. They had also gotten along well on a vacation to Nevada and Arizona, and would walk around holding hands.

"It was like they were dating," he said.

Not long before Bonny's murder, Caldwell said, Blake had received a call from director Bernardo Bertolucci, who had made *Last Tango in Paris* with Marlon Brando back in the 1970s. Blake had been excited that they might be working together on a film project. He said that Blake had begun working out at a gym he had set up inside his home, getting himself "camera ready" for possible movie roles that he was hoping to get. He also said that Blake adored Rose, but

Bakley did not show much interest in the baby girl. Caldwell said that he had no doubt about Blake's innocence in his wife's murder.

"I'm so convinced Robert had nothing to do with it," he said. "I'll say that to my dying day."

CHAPTER 17

ACCORDING TO THOSE WHO KNEW ROBERT BLAKE and his first wife, Sondra Kerr, Sondra was terrified of her husband and lived in near-constant fear of him. This seemed especially true during their final years together after Blake accused her of having an affair with actor Steve Railsback while they were working on the television movie *Helter Skelter* together in 1976. Railsback portrayed Charles Manson.

"It was the only time she broke her marriage vows after nearly twenty years as a devoted and loyal wife despite Blake's affairs with many actresses," a friend of Sondra's told reporters. "But he couldn't take it. I think the idea of her in the arms of another man drove him crazy. She forgave him for all his waywardness, but he couldn't forgive her."

According to Sondra's friend, their 1982–83 divorce dispute was bitter, and was centered around alimony and custody of the children, as most divorces are. But their battle was short-lived, purportedly because Blake had intimidated Sondra into giving up the children and most of the marital assets as well.

According to the *Globe*, a friend of Sondra alleged, "He soon persuaded her to see things his way. He simply terrorized her into giving him total custody of their two kids. Once, when she told me that she tried to see them, he forced a gun in her mouth and then to her head, and screamed, 'If you try to see them again, I'll blow your head off!' She was absolutely terrified of him because he had threatened to kill her on more than one occasion. I think he got his way over custody and the divorce settlement by pure intimidation. He kept the kids and barred her from seeing them again and kept virtually all of their assets."

On another occasion Blake purportedly held a loaded gun to Sondra's head and forced her to tell their children that she did not love them and that she wanted them to remain with their father.

"Not being able to see her children broke Sondra's heart," her friend said. "Blake poisoned their minds, convincing them that she was the cause of their breakup because of her infidelity with Railsback. He told them their mother was a whore and they must never see her again."

According to Sondra's friends, the physical and mental abuse that was allegedly inflicted upon her by Blake over the years nearly destroyed her, both spiritually and financially.

"Sondra says that from the time the kids were just babies, things were not well with her and Robert," one of her friends told reporters. "He cheated on her and treated her terribly. He was using drugs, abusing alcohol, and trying to come to grips with his fame. All the while Sondra was at home, trying to protect their babies. But she didn't want to leave him. It was a classic case of keeping the family together for the sake of the children."

Prior to their divorce, Sondra had a promising career in television and the movies. After the divorce, however, her career took a nose-dive from which it did not recover. She rented a small apartment in Studio City, not far from where Bonny Lee Bakley was murdered. The children were still small and she could try to keep an eye on them and occasionally see them if they happened to pass by. She was otherwise not allowed to see them, and didn't push the issue out of her fear of Blake.

According to the *Star*, a friend of Sondra's said, "To this day, Sondra is scared to death of Robert. She speaks about him only in very hushed tones. She's worked at a series of odd jobs and appears in small theater productions, always getting rave reviews. But she's never been able to put her life back together after what Robert did to her . . . Sondra told me that when she heard the news about Blake's new wife being murdered, a chill went down her spine. She said, 'I knew all along something like that could happen to me.'"

Shortly after the reports of Sondra's abusive relationship with Robert Blake came out, she called a news conference at the offices of her attorney, Gloria Allred. She said that she was not the source of all of the stories that had described her marriage as an abusive relationship, and would neither confirm nor deny the validity of those stories.

"I think it is important that it be known that I did not tell those stories," Sondra told the reporters at the news conference. "I'm not denying or saying they're true."

Often appearing near tears, Sondra said that the fact that she would not confirm or deny the reports, most of which appeared in supermarket tabloids, should not be taken as lending credibility to those reports. Allred stepped in and said that if her client commented on the abuse allegations, it could cause problems.

"She's not going to open up a Pandora's box," Allred said, but did not elaborate.

Prior to the news conference, Sondra had appeared on NBC's *Today* show and had recalled what her marriage to Blake had been like in vague detail.

"It was a lengthy marriage," she said, "and like all marriages it had its ups and downs." She would only say that there were "significant reasons" why the marriage failed, but she maintained that she wanted to keep those reasons private. "I do not wish to speak about my personal relationship with Robert at this time."

Despite the probing of reporters, Sondra refused to comment about whether Blake was innocent or guilty in his new wife's death. Instead, she would only say that it was a "horrible tragedy."

"I was in shock," she said of the murder. "It evokes deep sadness and upset. My heart goes out to the baby and to the family."

Meanwhile, as Robert Blake remained in seclusion, yet another secret from Bonny Bakley's past surfaced. Apparently there was another husband that no one had heard anything about. An older man named Joseph Brooksher, who lives in a rural area near Frankford, Missouri, came forward and revealed that he was Bakley's husband. His revelation also indicated that he and Bonny may not have been legally divorced, a fact that brought into play considerable doubt as to whether Bonny and Blake's marriage was valid.

According to Brooksher, he and Bonny were married in November 1992 at a time when Bakley had been calling herself Bonny Lee Lewis. Brooksher said that his memories of his marriage to Bonny were not fond ones. He said that they had met through the mail and got married in Memphis about six months afterward. That, he said, had been the last time he had seen her.

"I didn't even see her after that," Brooksher said. "She left in the night. I didn't see her no more."

But there was more to the story than being abandoned on his wedding night. Brooksher said that he served four years in prison for bad checks that Bonny had written in his name. It was also revealed that their divorce was in doubt because the Tennessee court documents pertaining to the divorce had been filed, but Bonny apparently had never followed through with the proceedings. If that turned out to be the case, it would place the legality of her marriage to Blake in doubt, as well as any marriages in between Brooksher and Blake that remained undiscovered.

While the police continued to investigate Bonny Lee Bakley's murder, additional details about actor Gary Busey being on Bonny's "young and rich" list were revealed. According to reports, Busey was playing in a celebrity charity golf tournament in Palm Springs when he received a call from Harland Braun, also a lawyer for Busey, telling him that he was at the top of Bonny's list of potential victims.

"She targeted Gary Busey," Braun said. He explained that Bonny had written to Busey's mother, who handles the actor's fan mail, in an attempt to obtain Busey's address and telephone number in Los Angeles. "She had a list of people she was going after and his name was down for March 30, 2001."

For reasons that were not known, Bonny had not fulfilled her plan. Busey told Braun that he had not heard from Bakley, and said that he did not know if she had actually spoken to his mother or not.

As details of Bonny's many marriages continued to surface, providing the LAPD detectives with even more leads to follow up on, it was revealed that she had been married to an 83-year-old Florida man, William Weber Sr., at one point. The marriage had been a short one, like many of the others. The victim's conservator, however, had promptly annulled this one.

Weber, it turned out, had met Bonny through a lonely hearts magazine. He had answered the ad, and Bonny began sending him letters immediately. Before Weber's relatives knew what was going on, Bonny had already gone to his house. They were married the next day. Two nights later, Bonny left unexpectedly from the second-floor window in his Florida condominium, but not before she had obtained access to his bank account. Before Weber's conservator and his bank could put a freeze on his account, $350,000 had been withdrawn and Bonny had disappeared.

Meanwhile, Anthony Helm, who had been Bonny Bakley's Memphis attorney, revealed that his office had been broken into. Strangely, the only things missing were about a dozen pornographic photos of Bakley that had been removed from her file—many of the same photos that she offered for sale in the ads she placed—and the legal office's telephone log of calls received. The photos had been practically worthless when Bonny was alive, but after her murder they had become considerably more valuable.

"Indirectly," Helm said, "I got an offer from a tabloid through an attorney. It involved $100,000 for the photos." Helm said that he turned down the offer.

"I may have been a little bit naive," he said of the heist, "but first of all this is a bank building—there's pretty good security here."

As the investigation moved slowly forward, it was apparent that the LAPD investigators were working with few clues as they attempted to solve Bonny's murder. Even though the detectives had initially accused Blake of committing the murder, going so far as to ask when and where he committed the crime, they seemed just as baffled nearly two weeks after her murder as they were when they initially tried to reconstruct the events that led up to her death. Blake's identification as a prime suspect, as well as various accusations about him killing his wife at a different location, were blasted by his attorney, Harland Braun.

"It doesn't make any sense," Braun said. "They were telling him that he took her away, killed her somewhere else, and then brought her back. What I found astounding about this is that it wouldn't make any sense from the time line."

The long and the short of it all seemed to be that, two weeks into the case, the LAPD investigators were not any closer to making an arrest than they were the night of the murder.

CHAPTER 18

The National Enquirer soon revealed that it had received secret tapes that Bonny had recorded of her conversations with Robert Blake and others. The tabloid obtained the tapes from members of Bonny's family. They apparently depicted Blake's rage over her pregnancy and her refusal to get an abortion. LAPD detectives learned of the tapes at about the same time the tabloid magazine planned to publish excerpts from them. According to *The National Enquirer's* editor-in-chief, Steve Coz, the publication did not pay for the tapes and they planned to turn them over to the investigators.

By the time the tapes were turned over to the investigators, excerpts had already been published in the tabloid and they were being played on radio and television news programs as well as over the Internet. Perhaps the most damning aspect of the tapes was that they depicted a side of Robert Blake that most people had not seen, and they provided a reasonably strong motive for killing his wife. Braun conceded that the tapes were probably reasonably consistent with what Blake and Bonny had been discussing at the time they were made, but he stressed that they didn't mean that he had killed his wife.

"He has a motive," Braun said. "But so do a lot of other people. Robert said to me a few days ago, 'As long as the police don't try to fabricate evidence, I have nothing to worry about.' "

The tapes, recorded in the early part of 2000, depicted Blake accusing Bonny of deliberately getting pregnant and reneging on an earlier promise in which she had apparently agreed to get an abortion.

"That was a rotten, stinking, filthy lie!" Blake said.

During the first phone calls between them, Blake could be heard making plans to take Bonny to an abortion clinic.

"We're gonna go to the clinic and get that out of the way," Blake said. "You get your legs shaved, get all perked up. I'm gonna take you up there at eight A.M."

However, Blake never showed up, and could be heard later complaining of pain from colon and prostate cancer. He told Bonny that he had spent the night in a hospital because he'd had a reaction to chemotherapy. His claims of having cancer were believed to have been a lie.

"The therapy just wears me out," Blake said. "I guess I'm lucky my hair hasn't fallen out. If this surgery doesn't work out, the end of the trail is just a couple years off for me. Anyway, sweetheart, I'll see you between three and four o'clock today unless you don't hear from me because somebody shot me!"

"What?" Bakley asked, obviously shocked by his statement.

"No, I'm just teasing," Blake assured her.

The next time Blake called, Bonny told him that she didn't think she could go through with the abortion, sending Blake into a rage.

"There's a pill you can take, if you want," Blake told her.

"Couldn't I just maybe give temporary custody to my mother or something?" Bonny asked.

"Have the baby and give it to your mother?" Blake asked. "Why? What would that do?"

"Because you don't want it around you."

"I'd rather you didn't have it," Blake told her, after which Bonny began crying.

"Why can't you let me be with you and I'll make my mother watch it?" Bonny asked.

"You know if you are going to do it, you have to do it really soon," Blake said.

"I don't want to do it!"

"You know all those crazy letters you wrote me. You already knew you were pregnant and all that stuff," Blake said as he grew more enraged. "You are who you are and you do what you do. If that's the way you can live and you can live with yourself doing stuff like that, it's gonna come down on you!"

"All I wanted is to be with you. I didn't know there was anything wrong."

"Deliberately getting pregnant is wrong. Writing letters to me about how you are going to get an abortion. You promised me. You said, 'I'll take pills. You don't have to worry, if I ever get pregnant, I swear on my life I'll get an abortion.' How can you lie to me like that?" Blake shouted furiously.

"Don't do this!" Bonny pleaded.

"I'm not the bad guy here. I didn't lie. I didn't cheat. I didn't hustle. I didn't do anything wrong!"

"You never lied?" Bonny asked. "What about the

time you said you were too sick to go do that show
and afterwards I found out you did."

"You got it all figured out in your head already,"
Blake charged. "Getting pregnant deliberately and lying to me about abortions. That's who you are and
that's what you do and that is the name of that tune!"

"You don't understand," Bonny said. "I figured that
maybe there would be a better connection between
us."

"Oh yeah," Blake said. "Getting pregnant when it
is the one thing I'm terrified of, that's gonna be a
better connection. You lied to me, you double-dealt
me and that's who you are!" Blake began yelling into
the phone. "You promised me! You said, 'Don't
worry Robert, no matter what. I'll have an abortion.'
And it was all a lie!"

"If you don't want me out here, I won't . . ." Bonny
trailed off, crying.

"You swore to me on your life that no matter what,
I didn't have to worry, and that was a rotten, stinking,
filthy lie and you deliberately got pregnant. Your period ended on August 20 and you were out here fucking me on the exact day you were supposed to. For
the rest of your life you'll have to live with that and
for the rest of my life I'll never forget it!"

"People hurt each other all the time," Blake said,
at a different point in the tape. "But when you hurt
somebody deliberately, somebody you care about, rip
their fucking heart out, make them crawl and squirm,
that's tough stuff. I mean, you have to live with yourself, and I don't know how you do it . . . The one
thing in the world you knew I was terrified of was

anybody getting pregnant, and you did it deliberately. Why? Not because you wanted to be with me. It has something to do with some crazy shit that's going on in your head that you want Robert Blake's baby. And that's all on you, baby, and *you* have to live with that. You schemed this whole thing!"

Bonny voiced a few words of protest and claimed that she was innocent of his charges, saying that all she wanted was to be with Blake.

"If you wanted to be with me, all you had to do is be with me. Yeah, I'm neurotic and crazy and I disappear from time to time, but I always come back and you know that."

"What about now?" Bonny asked.

"Baby, the ball is in your court. I've told you, I know who you are and I know *what* you are . . . You think you can hold this over my head and say you gotta be with me because you're pregnant."

It wasn't long after the tape recordings of the telephone conversations between Blake and Bonny were released to the media, as well as to the police, that additional letters that Bonny had written to Blake came out. The letters provided some insight into how Bonny appeared to be plotting to profit from her relationship with Blake. Some people, including Bonny's ex-husband, Paul Gawron, believed the letters may have contributed to her death.

"I believe that Bonny was writing her own obituary with these letters," Gawron said. "She was blackmailing him and putting so much pressure on Blake that she pushed him to the brink. I believe these letters led to her murder. She was messing with a guy you shouldn't mess with. She tricked him and was rubbing it in his face."

In return for giving up any rights to Blake's $8 million estate by signing a prenuptial agreement that, ultimately, was never signed, Bonny sent a letter to Blake saying that she wanted a ring. She told him to "make it at least a carat, size 6 . . . as long as it's real."

In another letter she threatened that if Blake wanted her to stay away from his fortune, he had to marry her because she did not want to split up with Christian Brando for anything less than marriage.

"After all," she wrote, "it may not just be your money I'd miss out on by marrying you. It might be Marlon's as well, via Christian someday."

In a letter to Cary Goldstein, who had represented her earlier, Bonny began questioning the legality of her marriage to Blake. She said that he had signed the marriage license with his given name, Michael James Gubitosi, instead of his legal name, Robert Blake, and wanted to know if that was legal. She charged that Blake had not consummated the marriage.

"So that alone makes it not legal, doesn't it?" she asked Goldstein. She also indicated that she wanted to sue Blake for fraud. "Let's get him," she told Goldstein.

It seemed reasonably clear from her letters that Bonny wanted more than marriage out of Robert Blake. It appeared that he had been targeted, probably all along, as a victim in one of her schemes.

In one letter Bonny told Blake that she was using birth-control pills when, in fact, she was taking fertility drugs, a fact confirmed by her daughter, Holly.

Later she writes to him to tell him that the pills hadn't worked after she learned that she had become pregnant.

"I hate to tell you this," she wrote, "but the pill did not work for me. I was supposed to take them for a week or two at first. I didn't start them until a couple days before [we had sex]."

Despite the fact that Blake had previously told her that he was terrified of her becoming pregnant, in at least one letter she taunts him by telling him she might want to have another child with him.

"Forget the vasectomy or any means of birth control," she wrote, in reference to a recent conversation. "All that stuff just turns me off. In fact I may want to try for another [child]."

By the time Blake had figured out that Bonny was a con artist, it was too late, since she was already pregnant. Nonetheless, he brought in his lawyers and a private detective to help him with his dilemma. It was then that he learned all about her shady background, and it became evident that he clearly did not want to be with Bonny. She apparently knew how he felt now, and she resorted to writing letters to Blake asking that he call off the lawyers. When Blake refused, her letters became a little nastier.

"Maybe it's for the best," she wrote. "[The lawyers] are trying so hard to convince you I'm out for something. That sort of evens it out a bit because I've been convinced you just want to save on child support. If they are going to scrutinize everything I do, then they are the ones going to cost you."

She told Blake that she had no conscience.

"I don't even know why I do half the things I do," she wrote, a statement that could be construed as a veiled threat of sorts.

A line from a poem Bonny wrote seemed to say everything that needed to be said about her value system: "When it comes to cars I like a Cadillac. It's the only way you're gonna get me in the sack."

CHAPTER 19

BY MID-MAY BONNY LEE BAKLEY'S BODY WAS STILL unclaimed at the Los Angeles County Morgue. Funeral plans remained in limbo as the LAPD continued its investigation into her murder. By then Bonny's relatives were literally begging for her body to be released and sent home to them so they could finally lay her to rest, all the while waiting, and expecting, Robert Blake to foot the bill.

According to Scott Carrier, a spokesman for the Los Angeles County Coroner's office, Bonny's sister, Margerry, was in town and was planning to ask Blake for the right to claim Bonny's body from the third-floor refrigerated storage unit where it had been lying since the autopsy.

"They have come here to make a plea to Mr. Blake, because they have no money," Carrier said.

According to the county coroner's policy, the spouse of the deceased has first rights to claim the body. Harland Braun stated the reason that Bonny's body had not been claimed by Blake: He had been unable to obtain an autopsy report due to the records having been sealed by the authorities. Depending on what was stated in the report, Braun said that he might advise Blake to order a private autopsy.

On Wednesday, May 16, arrangements were made to release Bonny's body to Armstrong Mortuary in

Los Angeles, where Blake had scheduled a small religious service for his slain wife. It wasn't known whether the coroner's office had released the results of Bonny's autopsy to Harland Braun's office or not, or whether Braun had obtained the private independent autopsy he had referred to earlier. Everyone associated with the case remained tight-lipped. Only the details of the planned service were released.

However, an hour or so before the service was scheduled to begin, Braun received a telephone call from his investigator at Armstrong Mortuary. He told Braun that because of the throng of news media trying to cover the service, the funeral director was unable to get close enough to the building to bring Bonny's corpse inside.

Helicopters hovered overhead, and camera crews and reporters crowded against one other as each tried to get into position for the best shots of Blake and the casket cantaining Bakley's body. It was literally a mess. The fact that the coroner could not deliver Bonny's body prompted Blake and Bakley's family to cancel the service.

"We had a private religious service planned," Braun said. "A priest was coming and Robert was going to be there with his three children. But now we're afraid if he showed up there would be a riot . . . we have to look out for the living and we're afraid someone might get hurt . . . I've never seen anything like this. The emotions in this case are running so high."

Braun said that it had been Blake's intention to have a small, dignified service for Bonny before having her body released for shipment to New Jersey, where her family had made plans to hold a funeral service for her. Blake had indicated that he was considering going to the funeral in New Jersey.

"I'm going to advise him against going," Braun said.

After the service was canceled, Blake and Bonny's family issued a joint announcement that the body would be buried later on an undisclosed date, and at an undisclosed location, likely in New Jersey. The statement also mentioned that the families understood that the media was just doing its job, but they requested some privacy in the matter.

On Thursday, May 24, not quite three weeks since Bonny had been shot to death, Blake announced through his attorney that he would be burying her on Friday, May 25, at Forest Lawn Memorial Park in Hollywood Hills, a cemetery where many famous movie stars and other celebrities such as Bette Davis, Lucille Ball, Liberace, Roy Campanella, Don Drysdale, and others are buried. After consultation with Bonny's family, the decision was reached to have her buried in California. A media throng similar to the one that had shown up in Los Angeles surrounded the funeral home in New Jersey after hearing of the body's arrival time, prompting *that* service to be canceled. Braun said that Blake had made all of the funeral arrangement and was paying for the service. A Catholic priest would officiate. In addition to Blake, his adult children would attend the funeral, and Rose would be present. About a dozen relatives and friends would also attend.

"It'll be brief, but it is the kind of thing that has to be done," Braun said. "Robert is extremely saddened . . . He wanted to do this out of respect for the mother of his daughter and thankfulness that Rosie is in the world because of Bonny."

Blake also invited Bonny's family to attend the service and offered to pay for their transportation to and from California. However, the family declined the offer through their attorney, Cary Goldstein.

"There's a discomfort being around Mr. Blake and it'll essentially be a public relations event for him," Goldstein said. "They don't want to support that." Goldstein also said that there was a level of unease that the family felt about being around Blake. "They are reluctant to attend in the presence of Mr. Blake."

"I can't fathom it," Braun said. "They were invited and Robert even offered to pay their way out if money was an issue, but they've decided not to come.

"The problem is that if you don't alert people, the word gets out and it's even more chaotic," Braun continued, explaining why the details of the Forest Lawn service were not kept secret. He said that the public would not be allowed through the cemetery gates, and only invited media would be in attendance, although he would allow other media representatives time for questions at the cemetery's entrance.

On Friday morning, three weeks to the day since Bonny's murder, Robert Blake arrived at Forest Lawn Cemetery at 8:15 A.M., 45 minutes before the service was scheduled to begin. Looking straight ahead, he rode in a white sport utility-vehicle that carried him quickly past a crowd of reporters and photographers at the gate. Blake's daughter, Delinah, sat next to him and held the baby, Rose. He and Braun engaged in small talk and discussed legal strategy as they waited for the ceremony to begin.

Dressed in a dark suit, Blake looked haggard and grim as he made his first public appearance since Bonny's murder. Blake stood at graveside and spoke softly for about a minute as he fondly recalled his wife.

"It's because of Bonny that Rosie was born," Blake said as he delivered the brief eulogy. "It's because of her will and her conviction, not mine, and her dedication, not mine, that brought Rosie into this world. I thank God and I thank Bonny. I stand here before God, and I make this pledge: As long as He gives me breath, I will do everything I can to make our daughter Rosie's life the best that I can. I know that's what Bonny would want. I promise, promise you that. Bonny, I promise you."

Depending upon how one took it, the emphasis on promises was reminiscent of the taped conversations between Bonny and Blake, and that was chilling.

Blake thanked Bonny's family for allowing her burial in Los Angeles, where Rose could visit her mother's grave. As he left the graveside, Blake reached atop her casket and took a single white rose from the floral arrangement.

Afterward, Bonny's family issued an angry statement through their attorney.

"There is no unity between the Bakley family and

Mr. Blake," Goldstein said. "Certain members feel certain that Mr. Blake is responsible for the death of Leebonny. We believe the funeral staged by Mr. Blake to be nothing more than a public-relations event for him and his attorneys."

Harland Braun took exception to the statement and responded that the service was dignified.

"There was nothing staged about it," Braun said. He also expressed surprise at the Bakley family's attitude about boycotting the funeral. "To me, if a mother, a sister, a father dies, you go, period."

"I didn't feel I ought to stand next to the man I believe, strongly, killed my sister," Margerry Bakley told the Fox News Channel in an interview in New York after the service. She said that she did not want to associate with Blake, and criticized him for not following the wishes of her family to have Bonny cremated. "There's no love at that funeral." She said that Blake had a "script written out" for Bonny. "This is the end of the script, at least for her."

Margerry Bakley also said that she would seek custody of Rose, "if and when Robert Blake goes to jail." She also complained that she never gave her permission to hold the funeral in California.

She stated that when Bonny and Blake took the trip to Sequoia National Park, she believed that "the whole time he was going to kill her. It was just a matter of time." Four days after they returned, Bonny was murdered.

"I think he did this himself," Margerry said. "He hated my sister. I think he enjoyed doing it himself. I guess he covered his tracks very well." She said that the funeral was "the biggest screenplay he has ever written.

"Bonny fulfilled her fantasy of marrying a movie star," Margerry went on. "She thought they would live happily ever after even though she knew in the back of her head it would never happen. It wasn't right from the beginning."

AFTERWORD

ON JUNE 1, 2001, IT WAS REVEALED THAT ROBERT Blake and his attorneys had dispatched a team of investigators to various locations across the country to further investigate Bonny Lee Bakley's past, as well as her relatives' pasts. They were sent to New Jersey, Tennessee, Arkansas, and Mississippi to uncover whatever they could, scandalous or not, that might help the LAPD focus their investigation in a direction other than Blake's. Cary Goldstein said that he, as well as Bonny's relatives, could not understand why Blake "is devoting so much effort to further trashing his deceased wife."

"Blake's private investigators are here in New Jersey [and other states] speaking to anyone who has known Bonny or I," said Margerry Bakley, who remained in the Garden State after much of her family moved to Arkansas. "The investigators have spoken to two people that I know of . . . and all these guys are concerned with is digging up any or all things I have done in my past to present, [and they are doing the same to] Bonny's two adult children and basically any relative."

Harland Braun defended his and Blake's actions by saying that it was necessary because the LAPD is focusing its murder probe solely on Blake. "The LAPD is doing the Robert Blake part of the investigation,"

Braun said, "but is refusing to look anywhere else. We're supplementing it with our own investigation."

On June 4, 2001, a month to the day that Bonny was murdered, Robert Blake returned to his home in Studio City after being in seclusion at an undetermined location since the weekend of Bonny's death. It was generally believed that he had been staying at his daughter's home in Hidden Hills. "He's going to go about his business as normally he would and ignore the press," Braun said. "If he didn't, he'd become a prisoner himself."

Although a month had passed since Bonny's slaying, her murder remained an unsolved mystery as investigators continued to struggle with evidence and leads that might point them toward the perpetrator.

"The reality is that murder cases aren't wrapped up in a hurry," said Sergeant John Pasquariello, an LAPD spokesman. "It takes a long time to put all the pieces together. This is certainly not a closed investigation. But this is a case with a lot of little bits and pieces and it may take a while. We're plodding along."

"We're doing a parallel investigation," Braun said. "They're investigating Robert and we're investigating everything else. We're not letting the trail go cold. Maybe we'll get lucky."

In the meantime the supermarket tabloid, *The Star*, offered Blake $100,000 to take a polygraph test to clear himself of suspicion in his wife's murder. "If Mr. Blake has nothing to hide, what better way is there of removing the umbrella of suspicion?" said *Star* editor-in-chief Tony Frost. "The results of a polygraph are not admissible in a court of law, but they do go a long way to convincing the court of public opinion."

If Blake agreed, he would be asked four questions: Did he kill Bakley? Does he know who killed her? Did he arrange the killing? Did he have access to a Walther handgun?

Similarly, a Los Angeles radio station, KFI-AM, offered Blake $64,000 if he would take a polygraph test administered by someone chosen by the station.

Blake has passed on both offers.

During the first week of June, it was announced that LAPD detectives had expressed interest in re-examining two audiotape statements Blake made to the police about the night Bonny was murdered. One of the tapes was made during an interview with Blake on the night of the murder, and the other was made when he was called in for a second interview. Blake apparently told officers that he felt responsible for his wife's death because he had left her alone. The detectives also planned to check the 911 call Blake made from Sean Stanek's house, in which he purportedly stated that his wife had been beaten up.

On Friday, June 8, 2001, LAPD detectives flew to Monroe, Louisiana to speak with Frankie Jean Lewis, a friend of Bonny's and the younger sister of singer Jerry Lee Lewis. Lewis apparently told a Monroe television station that she had a cell-phone conversation with Bonny only minutes before she was murdered, according to CBS 2 News.

"That evening she was telling me about what they

had eaten and that was not normal for Bonny," Lewis said. "It was more of a rattling conversation, more of a rambling, more of a 'I don't know what else to say, he's . . . coming back to the car' and that was it." Lewis said that Bonny had told her on the phone, " 'I'm waiting' and 'I won't be able to talk long.' "

Braun, however, told reporters that he had possession of Bakley's cell-phone records and they discredited Lewis's claims.

The investigators said that if Lewis can provide enough solid information, it might be enough to bring Blake in for more questioning. However, that has not occurred, yet.

Finally, it should be remembered that Robert Blake, though being investigated in his wife's murder, has not been charged with any crime relating to her death and as such should be afforded the same presumption of innocence that would be afforded someone who had been charged with a crime. For now, this story has no ending.

Appendix

FILMOGRAPHY OF ROBERT BLAKE

Pretty as a Picture: The Art of David Lynch (1997) (TV)

Lost Highway (1997)

Money Train (1995)

Judgment Day: The John List Story (1993) (TV)

Heart of a Champion: The Ray Mancini Story (1985) (TV)

"Hell Town" (1985)

Father of Hell Town (1985) (TV)

Murder One, Dancer 0 (1983) (TV)

Blood Feud (1983) (TV)

Joe Dancer: The Big Trade (1981) (TV)

Second-Hand Hearts (1981)

Of Mice and Men (1981) (TV)

Monkey Mission, The (1981) (TV)

Coast to Coast (1980)

Baretta (1975) (TV)

Busting (1974)

Electra Glide in Blue (1973)

Corky (1972)

Uomo dalla pelle dura, L' (1971)

Tell Them Willie Boy Is Here (1969)

In Cold Blood (1967)

This Property Is Condemned (1966)

Greatest Story Ever Told, The (1965)

"Richard Boone Show, The" (1963) (TV)

PT 109 (1963)

Town Without Pity (1961)

Purple Gang, The (1960)

Battle Flame (1959)

Pork Chop Hill (1959)

Beast of Budapest, The (1958)

Revolt in the Big House (1958)

Tijuana Story, The (1957)

Rumble on the Docks (1956)

Screaming Eagles (1956)

Three Violent People (1956)

Rack, The (1956)

Veils of Bagdad, The (1953)

Apache War Smoke (1952)

Black Rose, The (1950)

Black Hand (1949)

Treasure of the Sierra Madre, The (1948)

Homesteaders of Paradise Valley (1947)

Last Round Up, The (1947)

Marshal of Cripple Creek (1947)

Return of Rin-Tin-Tin, The (1947)

Rustlers of Devil's Canyon, The (1947)

Oregon Trail Scouts (1947)

Vigilantes of Boomtown (1947)

California Gold Rush (1946)

Conquest of Cheyenne (1946)

Guy Could Change, A (1946)

In Old Sacramento (1946)

Out California Way (1946)

Sheriff of Redwood Valley (1946)

Humoresque (1946)

Stagecoach to Denver (1946)

Santa Fe Uprising (1946)

Sun Valley Cyclone (1946)

Home on the Range (1946)

Great Stagecoach Robbery (1945)

Horn Blows at Midnight, The (1945)

Lone Texas Ranger, The (1945)

Marshal of Laredo (1945)

Pillow to Post (1945)

Wagon Wheels Westward (1945)

Dakota (1945)

Colorado Pioneers (1945)

Phantom of the Plains (1945)

Cheyenne Wildcat (1944)

Meet the People (1944)

Sheriff of Las Vegas (1944)

Vigilantes of Dodge City (1944)

Woman in the Window, The (1944)

Big Noise, The (1944)

San Antonio Kid, The (1944)

Marshal of Reno (1944)

Dancing Romeo (1944)

Tale of a Dog (1944)

Radio Bugs (1944)

Calling All Kids (1943)

Little Miss Pinkerton (1943)

Lost Angel (1943)

Salute to the Marines (1943)

Slightly Dangerous (1943)

Three Smart Guys (1943)

Election Daze (1943)

Farm Hands (1943)

Family Troubles (1943)

Benjamin Franklin, Jr. (1943)

Andy Hardy's Double Life (1942)

China Girl (1942)

Kid Glove Killer (1942)

Mokey (1942)

Rover's Big Chance (1942)

Unexpected Riches (1942)

Mighty Lak a Goat (1942)

Doin' Their Bit (1942)

Surprised Parties (1942)

Don't Lie (1942)

Going to Press (1942)

Melodies Old and New (1942)

1-2-3 Go! (1941)